The

ESSENTIAL

Gardening
Made Easy

Creative
CONTAINER
Gardens

INTERNATIONAL
MASTERS
PUBLISHERS, INC.

C O N T E N T S

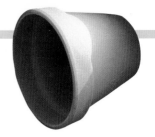

WELCOME

The ESSENTIAL
Gardening Made Easy
Creative Container Gardens

THE JOY OF GARDENING in containers is that anyone can do it, and you can grow a garden any time of the year and practically anywhere! Container gardening can be as easy as the several days it takes to sprout herb seeds in the kitchen or as time-consuming as growing a miniature Bonsai tree that could be tended to for several centuries. For most of us, container gardening falls somewhere in between these two extremes.

Urban gardeners are already familiar with the concept of growing container plants on balconies and terraces, but even rural residences can be transformed with dynamic windowboxes, hanging baskets on porches, and welcoming entryway planters. From traditional flower pots to unique wagons and barrels, the "Ideas and Inspirations" section will highlight the wide range of containers available for small-scale garden schemes. Planters can be designed to be placed on the ground, carted on wheels for a portable garden, or mounted on walls to adorn architectural elements.

To find the best container for a particular gardening situation, turn to the "Tasks and Techniques" section. Discover the proper way to care for and maintain containers, purchase pot-grown plants, prepare potting mix, and repot overcrowded plants. You'll even learn how to make your own handsome and inexpensive "faux stone" containers.

Next, check the "Plant Guide" section for tips on selecting the best plants. Grow tender tropical plants like Calla Lilies outdoors in summer, then move them inside for winter. Or, fill a tub with summer annuals like Sweet Peas, and replace them in fall with a flurry of bright Mums. Container gardening gives you the chance to experiment with plants that you might not ordinarily consider, and is an easy way to add brilliant color to unexpected spaces.

a moveable bed of blooms

for inside and outdoors

GARDENING IN CONTAINERS seems second nature. Nearly everyone loves to have lush greenery and blooms in their house, and apartment dwellers have little choice for gardening except in containers. In many parts of the country, container gardening is the only practical way to grow tropical plants, like Bay Tree and Birds-of-Paradise, or to force spring bulbs to bloom out of season. The ability to move containers indoors and out both avoids frost damage and brightens interior living spaces.

Nearly any plant, at least when it is small, can be grown in a container. Even some shrubs and trees can be successfully grown in large tubs or barrels. In fact, it has become a popular trend to choose living Christmas trees for indoor use during the holiday season and then moving them outdoors or onto a porch for the rest of the year. Trees in containers can provide a tall, graceful backdrop for a patio or can soften the corners of an interior room. Discovering the fun of combining a selection of different heights and shapes of plants in a variety of unusual pots offers an inexpensive way to give a familiar room or front porch a whole new look.

The first step in container gardening is selecting containers that complement the plants you're displaying—matching plants' growth habits, shapes, and maximum height and spreads to the style and size of the container. Most annuals are easy to grow in pots, and small annuals like Sweet Alyssums, Edging Lobelias, and Ageratums can be grown in nearly any container 4 in. in diameter or greater. Tall-growing annuals like Sweet Peas and perennial climbers will need staking or supports and therefore require larger containers. If space is at a premium, consider growing bushier plant varieties such as 'Cupid' Sweet Pea, which is at home in smaller pots.

The material that a planter is made of is a very important feature to consider. Plastic, glass, metal, and glazed

transform a deck or porch with a colorful container garden

Edible container gardens are a delightful way to enjoy fresh herbs, fruits, and vegetables during the winter or where space is limited. Pressure-treated wood containers are not recommended for edibles, however, because the wood contains toxic metal salts.

Consider growing pot herbs like Thyme, Chives, and Dwarf Rosemary in containers near or in the kitchen. Pansies are easy to grow in containers and their edible flowers, present outdoors from spring through fall, can be enjoyed indoors during winter. In addition to being lovely, the intriguing and brightly colored foliage of Ornamental Kale is edible. Strawberries also make wonderful container plants. They are often grown in "strawberry jars": shapely terra-cotta containers with planting holes or "pockets" along their sides.

pottery are watertight and will hold soil's moisture longer than those made of porous materials, such as terra-cotta, unglazed clay, peat, faux stone, or cement. Porous pots require more frequent watering but, if small, can be periodically dunked in a bucket of water and soaked. Containers made of wood are very attractive and easy to paint, but can rot quickly if kept constantly moist. To increase the durability of your wooden planters, use plastic liners so that soil is not in direct contact with wood.

Ideal for showcasing trailing plants, hanging baskets are usually made of plastic or fashioned from wire frames and filled with unmilled sphagnum moss or coarse peat. Because they are more exposed to the elements, wire-frame baskets need frequent watering to prevent plants from drying out.

Regardless of the type of container you choose, good drainage is essential. Your container should have drainage holes, which can be loosely covered with pot shards, gravel, or screening to prevent soil from leaking out. It's also important to use a porous potting mix that allows water to flow freely through to the bottom. To avoid staining patio or porch surfaces with water, place your container on a tray.

Because they are not exposed to wind and direct sunlight, indoor container plants don't need to be watered as often as those placed outside. Water indoor containers only when the surface of the soil starts to dry out, since more indoor plants die of drowning and rotting than of dehydration.

GARDEN IDEAS & INSPIRATION

Ideas for Pastel
Colors for a Courtyard

Create a planting that is elegant year round by combining flowers in soft pastels that bloom in each season with attractive, evergreen foliage.

Soft, Elegant Colors

For a planting that is always attractive, mix long-blooming plants with plants offering handsome foliage all year.

Courtyards are typically high-traffic areas that need to look good in all seasons. With careful selection, you can create a display of flowers from early spring to fall. Selecting only plants with pastel blooms ensures the garden is always harmonious, no matter what the season. Evergreen plants are invaluable for year-round structure and winter color.

This garden features sun-loving plants that are fairly low-growing and need a minimum of special care such as staking. They will do well in average, well-drained soil. A gravel mulch will keep down weeds and looks attractive even during winter.

CALLA LILY
H: 1 ½-3 ft., S: 1 ½ ft.; dramatic, funnel-shaped, pure white flowers in early to mid-summer; dark green, arrow-shaped leaves; dig up before frost and overwinter indoors in cold climates; zones 8-11

MILKY BELLFLOWER
H: 3-4 ft., S: 2 ft.; clusters of pale lilac, white, or pink flowers in summer; narrow, oval leaves; zones 3-7

DIANTHUS 'DORIS'
H: 3-6 in., S: 10-12 in.; fragrant, double, pale salmon-pink flowers with dark "eyes" in summer; blue-green, evergreen leaves; zones 4-8

CRANESBILL
H: 10 in., S: 12 in.; mounds of single, cup-shaped flowers in pale to bright pink, white, lilac, or violet-blue in summer; deeply cut leaves; zones 3-8

ROSEMARY
H and S: 6 ft.; tiny, lavender-blue flowers in summer; shrubby herb with pungent, needle-like, gray-green leaves; grow in containers in cold climates; zones 8-9

POTENTILLA 'PRINCESS'
H: 3 ft., S: 5 ft.; white to pale pink flowers from late spring to fall; dark green, deeply divided leaves; zones 2-7

DIANTHUS 'PINK JEWEL'
H: 4 in., S: 8-10 in.; double, bright pink summer flowers; evergreen, blue-green leaves; zones 3-9

POLYANTHA ROSE 'THE FAIRY'
H and S: 2 ft.; sprays of double, light pink flowers in summer and fall; glossy leaves; zones 4-9

1 **Clear grass** from the courtyard. Dig up bricks or other building rubble. Spread 2 in. of compost and dig in to a depth of 1-2 ft.

2 **Plant Bellflowers** at the back of courtyard, 2 ft. apart. Plant clumps of Dianthus and Cranesbills 10-12 in. apart.

3 **Plant Potentilla** and Rose 3 ft. apart. Set the shrubs so roots are at the same depth they were in their nursery containers.

4 **After danger** of frost has passed, plant Calla Lily at back of garden. Bring out pot-grown Rosemary and tuck in ground near Dianthus.

5 **Spread newspaper** eight sheets thick to kill weeds, then cover with 1 in. of smooth gravel. Keep mulch away from plant stems.

6 **Dig up Calla Lily** before first frost. Store the roots in a frost-free place over winter. Prune Rose every spring to shape.

More Plants for a Pastel Courtyard

SEASON	PLANT	DESCRIPTION
SPRING	*Corydalis solida* *(far left)*	Clusters of mauve-pink flowers; gray-green leaves; 1 ft.; zones 5-8
	Hyacinth 'Delft Blue' *(left)*	Fragrant, pale blue flower clusters; strap-like leaves; 8 in.; zones 6-9
	Triumph Tulip 'Apricot Beauty'	Glowing, peach-pink blooms; strap-like leaves; 18 in.; zones 3-8
	Daffodil 'Salome'	Apricot-to-pink cups, white petals; strap-like leaves; 15 in.; zones 4-9
SUMMER	Blue Flax *(far left)*	Blue flowers on wiry stems; needle-like leaves; 1 ft.; zones 4-9
	Astilbe 'Snowdrift' *(left)*	White summer plumes; green, Fern-like foliage; 2 ft.; zones 3-9
	Dicentra eximia 'Zestful'	Sprays of deep rose pink flowers; Fern-like leaves; 18 in.; zones 3-9
	Daylily 'Fairy Tale Pink'	Pastel pink, ruffled flowers; strap-like leaves; 2 ft.; zones 3-9
FALL	Sedum 'Carmen' *(far left)*	Clusters of soft pink flowers; silver-green leaves; 2 ft.; zones 3-9
	Russian Sage 'Blue Spire' *(left)*	Sprays of violet-blue flowers; gray-green leaves; 3 ½ ft.; zones 4-9
	Reblooming Iris 'Late Lilac'	Rich lilac blooms in spring and fall; strap-like leaves; 2 ½ ft.; zones 3-9
	Allium 'Ozawa'	Spherical, rose-purple flowers; grass-like leaves; 9 in.; zones 4-8
EVERGREEN	Bearberry *(far left)*	Oval leaves; white summer flowers; red berries; 1 ft.; zones 2-8
	Liriope 'Lilac Beauty' *(left)*	Grass-like, dark green leaves; spikes of violet flowers; 1 ft.; zones 6-10
	Mahonia repens	Holly-like, evergreen leaves; yellow spring flowers; 1 ft.; zones 6-9
	Coral Bells 'Persian Carpet'	Silver-lined, purple leaves; greenish white flowers; 1 ft.; zones 4-9

Ideas for a Compact
Urban Terrace

To grow a wealth of flowers in a small space, cover walls with blooming vines and underplant with colorful flowers and container plants.

Successful Small Space Gardening

For a colorful garden that makes the most out of a compact space, select plants carefully and use them creatively.

Every inch of space counts in a small garden, so use a few tricks to create a long-lasting display. Train vines up trellises or walls to add height and color without taking up much room. To ensure a steady supply of flowers, select compact plants that either have extra-long bloom seasons or flower in different seasons.

Use pots to create an ever-changing display. Select a mix of containers, fill them with flowers, and rearrange as necessary to keep the brightest blooms at the forefront. Bring in new pots periodically to add color or change the look entirely.

CLEMATIS 'VILLE DE LYON'
H and S: 10-12 ft.; velvety-textured, carmine flowers with gold stamens from mid-summer to fall; leaves with three oval leaflets on twining stems; requires support; zones 3-8

CLEMATIS 'ETOILE VIOLETTE'
H and S: 10-12 ft.; showy, violet-purple blooms from mid- to late summer; leaves with three oval leaflets on twining stems; requires support; zones 3-8

CRANESBILL 'WARGRAVE PINK'
H: 1 ½ ft., S: 2 ft.; mounds of single, cup-shaped, pink flowers from early to late summer; lobed leaves; zones 4-8

PANSY 'UNIVERSAL WHITE BLOTCH'
H and S: 6-8 in.; rounded, white flowers from spring to early summer; low, dark green foliage; for longest bloom, pinch back spent flowers; annual; all zones

16

**PETUNIA
'PRIMETIME WHITE'**
H: 8-12 in.; S: 6-8 in.;
pure white, trumpet-
shaped blooms from
early summer to frost;
oval leaves; annual;
all zones

**VARIEGATED
CORNELIAN
CHERRY**
H: 10 ft., S: 12-15 ft.;
tiny, star-shaped,
yellow flowers in
early spring; dark
green, oval
leaves with
white edges;
zones 5-8

HOSTA
H and S: ½-3 ft.;
clump-forming
plants with
handsome, heart-
shaped leaves that
may be bright to
dark green, blue-
green, or variegated
with white or yellow;
clusters of pale lilac or
white flowers in summer
or fall; zones 3-9

1 Attach trellises to walls. Use 1 in. spacers to keep trellises slightly away from wall surface. Spread compost over bed and dig in.

2 Plant Clematis 1 ft. from base of trellis. Handle carefully to avoid breaking the delicate stems. Loosely tie stems to trellis.

3 Plant Cranesbills and Hostas in prepared bed 2 ft. apart and 2 ft. from base of wall. Mulch bed and water all plants thoroughly.

4 Fill containers with houseplant potting mix. Plant Cornelian Cherry, Pansies, and Petunias in pots and arrange at edge of bed.

5 Pinch back Pansies and Petunias and clip off spent flowers to encourage more blooms. Water pots every few days in summer.

6 When potted flowers begin to stop blooming, replace them with new pots filled with plants that are just starting to bloom.

More Compact Urban Courtyard Plants

TYPE			PLANT	DESCRIPTION
CLIMBERS			Morning Glory *(far left)*	Blue summer blooms; heart-shaped leaves; 10 ft.; annual; all zones
			Climbing Rose 'Dublin Bay' *(left)*	Double, red flowers all summer; dark green leaves; 12 ft.; zones 5-10
			Mina lobata	Red, tubular summer flowers; lobed leaves; 15 ft.; annual; all zones
			Primrose Jasmine	Yellow spring flowers; semi-evergreen leaves; 10 ft.; zones 8-10
CONTAINER PLANTS			Yellow Calla Lily *(far left)*	Gold summer flower cups; spotted leaves; 2 ft.; tender bulb; all zones
			Alpine Strawberry *(left)*	White late spring flowers; tasty fruit; evergreen leaves; 8 in.; zones 5-9
			Tuberous Begonia 'On Top'	Yellow flowers all summer; dark green leaves; 1 ft.; annual; all zones
			Datura 'Evening Fragrance'	Fragrant, white flowers in summer; oval leaves; 4 ft.; annual; all zones
FLOWERS			Cosmos 'Sonata Mixed' *(far left)*	Rose, red, or white summer flowers; lacy leaves; 2 ft.; annual; all zones
			Pink Tickseed *(left)*	Star-like, pink Daisies all summer; very thin leaves; 18 in.; zones 3-9
			Lavender 'Hidcote'	Lilac summer flowers; evergreen, gray-green leaves; 15 in.; zones 5-9
			Dicentra eximia 'Snowdrift'	White flowers from spring to fall; Fern-like foliage; 18 in.; zones 3-9
GROUNDCOVERS			Petunia 'Purple Wave' *(far left)*	Rose-purple spring to fall flowers; oval leaves; 6 in.; annual; àll zones
			Maiden Pink 'Zing Rose' *(left)*	Rose summer flowers; blue-green, evergreen foliage; 5 in.; zones 3-9
			Mazus reptans 'Alba'	White flowers in spring; oval leaves; spreading; 2 in.; zones 5-8
			Thyme 'Reiter Thyme'	Lavender summer flowers; aromatic, evergreen leaves; 3 in.; zones 4-9

Planting Colorful
Balcony Containers

Transform ordinary balconies into mini-gardens of welcome color with a few container plants.

PLANTING YOUR BALCONY CONTAINERS

YOU WILL NEED:

- ❏ Decorative wire frame, 30 in. long by 8 in. wide
- ❏ 6 terra-cotta pots
- ❏ 3 "L" pot brackets
- ❏ Wood screws
- ❏ Potting soil
- ❏ Peat moss
- ❏ Granular fertilizer

THE PLANTS:

- ❏ 1 Multiflora Petunia
- ❏ 2 Mound Petunias
- ❏ 2 Dalmation Bellflowers
- ❏ 4 Dianthus
- ❏ 2 Licorice Plants
- ❏ 2 Lobelias 'Rosamund'

Tip

Long-lasting performance from perennial plants in containers may require pruning roots on your established plants. After flowering, remove plants from pots, and trim roots if space in the container is limited. Replant in same pot with fresh soil or move the plant to a container that is 25 percent larger.

1 **Mount the metal frame** and "L" brackets to rails in a pleasing arrangement, using galvanized wood screws and washers for security.

2 **Fill all pots** with a combination of potting soil, peat moss, and granular fertilizer for a nutrient-rich, yet light, potting medium.

3 **Plant the containers** that fit into the metal frame. Plant the Multiflora Petunia in the oblong pot and one Lobelia in each side pot.

4 **For the central lower** pot, place the Licorice Plants at the back and drop in the Dianthus plants in front, just an inch or so apart.

5 **Plant each outside** lower pot with a Mound Petunia at the back and a Bellflower in front. Set onto metal clips below wire frame.

6 **Insert the pots** into the metal frame and position the lower central pot in its clip. Water all of the balcony containers thoroughly.

Above the Rest

*Aerial container gardens offer everything from living bouquets
to sit beside to flowering borders that artfully frame a distant view.*

INSIDE YOUR POTS

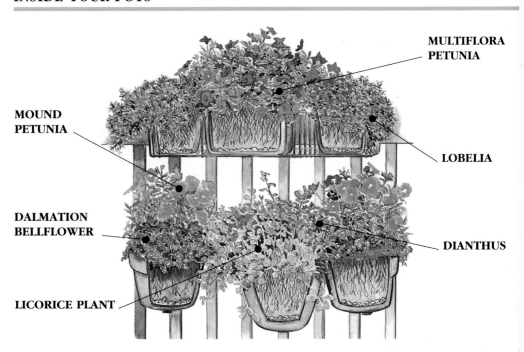

MULTIFLORA
PETUNIA

MOUND
PETUNIA

LOBELIA

DALMATION
BELLFLOWER

DIANTHUS

LICORICE PLANT

UPRIGHT PLANTS

● *Dianthus (above)* dresses up the container collection with tiny, delightfully fragrant flowers with delicate, fringed edges.
● *Mound Petunias* offer about the most reliable and vivid summer color around on plants that are well suited to virtually any container.

TRAILERS

● *Multiflora Petunias (above)*, often perennial plants in mild climates, are the star of this show with cascading, flowering stems.
● *Lobelias,* including this unusual 'Rosamund' variety in rose-pink, decorate the container edges with masses of tiny flowers.

FILLERS

● *Dalmation Bellflower (above)* is an ideal filler with low foliage and a mounding habit punctuated with bright flowers over many months.
● *Licorice Plant* gives subtle texture and color to the grouping with velvety, silver foliage that enhances the flowers.

Alternative Planting Ideas

ALL-IN-ONE GARDEN

This colorful rooftop container takes advantage of varied forms, foliage, and blooms of trees, shrubs, perennials, and annuals.

- 1 Crabapple tree
- 1 Shrubby Cinquefoil
- 1 Creeping Juniper
- 1 Geranium
- 1 Fan Flower
- 2 Pansies
- 3 Cosmos

AFTERCARE

On dry days in summer heat, container plants are likely to wilt. Prevent this, or help save those already showing signs of stress, by dunking the entire pot into a bucket of water. This also cools clay containers.

For year-round effect, especially on balconies with excellent views, use evergreens in containers. Many are hardy and can withstand urban conditions and they combine well with annuals and perennials.

OVER THE EDGE

A mixture of colors set off by the clean, white lines of this balcony makes this an attention-getting display. The plants combine bright blooms in a variety of textures and forms while foliage elements add interesting hues and shapes.

- 1 Geranium
- 2 Ageratums
- 2 Lobelias
- 2 Dusty Millers

ARRESTING IN RED

Dazzling red Impatiens steal the show in this balcony display featuring long-lasting, prolific Impatiens. Ideal in containers, these vibrant shade-lovers spill over the sides to make a complete floral bouquet.

- 12 red Impatiens
- 2 pink Impatiens
- 1 Lobelia
- 3 Ground Ivies

Add a burst of color to fading balcony containers quickly and easily with new annuals. Try new bloom colors and forms to give the planter even more appeal.

Planting a
Terra-cotta Wall Display

Create a unique vertical garden with these unusual containers brimming with color.

PLANTING YOUR POTS

YOU WILL NEED:

- ❏ 3 12 in. diameter terra-cotta wall pots
- ❏ Long bolts or screws (2 in. longer than hanging loop or hole of pot)
- ❏ Pliers or screwdriver
- ❏ Perlite
- ❏ Potting soil

THE PLANTS:

- ❏ 3 Statice 'Petite Bouquet'
- ❏ 1 Creeping Zinnia 'Gold Braid'
- ❏ 1 Baby's Breath 'Garden Bride'
- ❏ 1 Melampodium 'Showstar'
- ❏ 1 Blue Fanflower 'New Wonder'

Tip

Pots mounted on walls will get a double dose of heat, both directly from the sun and reflected from the wall itself. In addition, terra-cotta containers dry out more quickly than plastic ones. Check wall pots often for moisture by touching soil. Most will need watering daily in warm summer weather.

1 **Hold the pots** against the wall to plan arrangement and mark the location of each hole. Before planting, immerse pots in water for 15 minutes.

2 **Using markings** as a guide, attach screws (in wood walls) or molly bolts (in masonry) to mount pots so 3/4 in. protrudes inside pot.

3 **Add perlite** to bottom of each pot. Fill with potting soil. Plant Statice in left-hand corner of top pot and Creeping Zinnia next to it.

4 **In the middle pot,** plant the Baby's Breath on the left side and two Statice on the right side, leaving several inches between plants.

5 **In the lower pot,** plant the Melampodium on the left and the Blue Fanflower on the right, positioning it so that it spills over the pot rim.

6 **Gently firm** in plants; add more soil if needed. Add water until it drains out bottom and mount pots on wall over screws or bolts.

Off-the-wall Blossoms

Compact plants are displayed with style as they spill from elegant containers arranged on a wall.

INSIDE YOUR POTS

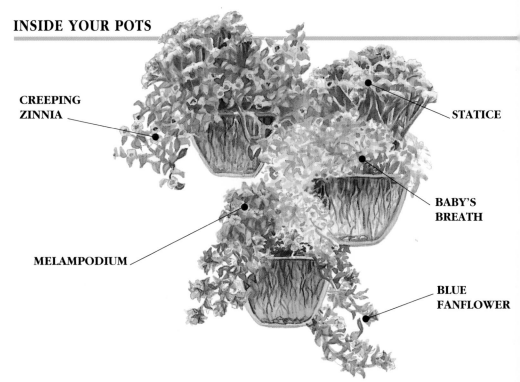

CREEPING ZINNIA

STATICE

MELAMPODIUM

BABY'S BREATH

BLUE FANFLOWER

UPRIGHT PLANTS

- **Statice** 'Petite Bouquet' *(above)* is an exceptionally easy annual offering strong stems of everlasting flowers in wonderful pastels.
- **Melampodium** 'Showstar' produces bushy mounds of perfectly formed, Daisy-like, golden flowers. It tolerates heat and drought.

TRAILERS

- **Creeping Zinnia** *(above)* blends well with almost everything. Handsome 'Gold Braid' sends out cascading stems topped with tiny, gold flowers with dark centers.
- **Blue Fanflower** 'New Wonder' has trailing stems of clustered, blue-violet flowers accented with yellow.

FILLER

- **Baby's Breath** *(above)* is unbeatable for a soft, lush look to fill in between other container plants. 'Garden Bride' is a new, dwarf form with tiny, pale pink and white, five-petaled flowers that float in a pastel cloud above mounds of lacy, cascading foliage.

Alternative Planting Ideas

ABOVE THE CROWD

Terra-cotta or ceramic wall planters create the ideal decoration for a wooden fence, single post, pillar, or even unadorned siding. Here, a cheerful combination of mixed pink Dianthus blends beautifully with ever-reliable, long-blooming, fragrant Sweet Alyssums.

- 6 mixed Dianthus
- 6 Sweet Alyssums

HOT COLORS

Bright pink and yellow heat up the color palette in this planting featuring a prolific Ivy Geranium decked out in abundant, hot pink blossoms and glossy, green leaves. Against a gold background, this single flower color becomes an arresting combination of warm colors in an eye-catching display.

- 1 pink Ivy Geranium

BLOOMING CURLS

Flowers spill like tendrils out of the top of this planter carved in the shape of a face. The reddish purple leaves of the Coral Bells are echoed in the trailing, violet blooms of Serbian Bellflowers, while the pinkish white blooms of Verbenas add highlights.

- 1 Coral Bells 'Palace Purple'
- 2 Serbian Bellflowers
- 2 Verbenas 'Peaches & Cream'

AFTERCARE

Give your plants a boost of liquid fertilizer every two to four weeks. Use fish emulsion or other organic products for safe, frequent feeding. Dilute the fertilizer in a watering can according to label directions; soak both the foliage and soil.

Periodically remove the pots from wall to inspect for cracks and to be sure the fasteners remain tightly affixed to wall. The end of each screw or bolt should protrude through mounting hole of each pot by at least 3/4 in. Brush away soil or debris on the wall behind where the pots hang, and look for damp spots. For better air circulation, place a small wooden block between each pot and wall.

Planting a
Sunny Windowbox

Add style to any window with a bouquet of summer flowers offering a hint of fragrance.

PLANTING A SUNNY WINDOWBOX

YOU WILL NEED:

❏ Windowbox, 34 in. wide,
  9 in. deep, 9 in. wide
❏ Bag of potting soil
❏ Fertilizer granules

THE PLANTS:

❏ 2 Salvias 'Blue Victoria'
❏ 2 Nicotianas 'Domino'
❏ 4 Lobelias
❏ 2 Classic Zinnias
❏ 1 Miniature Rose
  'Heartbreaker'
❏ 2 Marigolds 'Bonanza'

1 **Make sure your box** has proper drainage. Fill it with lightweight potting soil mixed with granular fertilizer to within an inch of the rim.

2 **Alternate Salvias** and Nicotianas as you plant them at the back of box. Leave enough space between them to allow for their mature size.

3 **Dig hole** the width of the Rose's roots spread out in box's center. Plant Rose so that the area where canes join main stem sits 1 in. higher.

4 **Loosen any tangled** roots of the Marigolds before planting them. Set the Marigolds to either side of the Miniature Rose.

Troubleshooter

Use galvanized steel "L" brackets at each end and in the center of windowboxes that are more than 2 ½ ft. long. To secure brackets, sink 3 in. wood screws into wood siding, and special anchor bolts into masonry.

Tip

Placing potted plants on plastic liners will prevent wooden boxes from rotting and allow you to change plants seasonally without having to replant.

5 **Plant Classic Zinnias** at each front corner of the windowbox. Position them near the edge so that the foliage can grow over the sides.

6 **Plant Lobelias** along left, right, and front sides of box. Plant them between the center and corner plants. Water box thoroughly.

Silky Summer Hues

Intensely colored flowers create an unusually beautiful look for a sunny, summer windowbox.

INSIDE YOUR WINDOWBOX

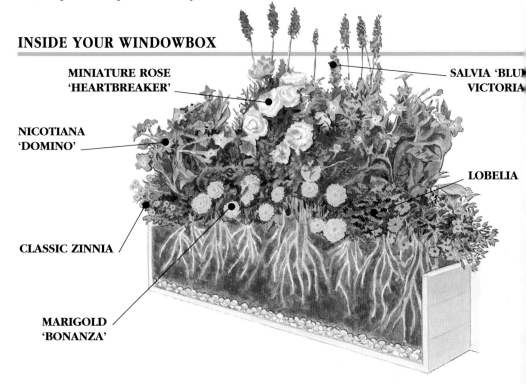

MINIATURE ROSE 'HEARTBREAKER'

SALVIA 'BLUE VICTORIA'

NICOTIANA 'DOMINO'

LOBELIA

CLASSIC ZINNIA

MARIGOLD 'BONANZA'

TRAILERS

- **Classic Zinnias** *(above)* bear bright yellow or white flowers and slender leaves that spill gracefully over the edge of the box.
- **Lobelia** offers tiny purple, lilac, white, or blue blooms from late spring until the first frost. Its foliage ranges from red bronzes to deep greens.

UPRIGHT PLANTS

- **Nicotiana** *(above)* is prized for its trumpet-shaped blooms. The white, pink, and scarlet flowers of 'Domino' provide long-lasting color.
- **Salvias**, such as this box's compact 'Blue Victoria', provide cool hues during hot summer months in spikes of blue, purple, or white.

FILLERS

- **Miniature Roses,** such as 'Heartbreaker' *(above)*, add a touch of class and an element of permanence to the box.
- **Marigolds** are easy-to-grow, dependable flowers in bright orange or gold hues. The 12 in. 'Bonanza' provides a nice transition between the spreading and upright plants.

Alternative Planting Ideas

CASCADES OF COLOR

A simple mix of blooms among profuse foliage can give a windowbox a lush feel. The foliage here adds the perception of depth.

- 2 Globe Amaranths
- 6 *Exacum affine*
- 4 Dahlberg Daisies
- 4 Verbenas
- 2 Rose Periwinkles
- 1 Trailing Lantana
- 1 Variegated Trailing Vinca

COTTAGE ELEGANCE

This design uses a tumble of flowers with thick, spreading foliage that softens the hard texture of the stone facade. The subtle flower colors offer a beautiful and elegant design that tranforms a stark, dark stone window into a soft and inviting garden.

- 6 Geraniums
- 2 Dracaenas
- 8 Petunias

A ROSY COMPLEXION

Incorporate a mix of trailing and erect flowering plants that offer shades of pink and rosy purple. Contrast these romantic hues with a ribbon of lemon yellow Wallflowers.

- 3 Rose Periwinkles
- 8 Yellow Wallflowers
- 5 Dusty Millers
- 8 Ivy-leaved Geraniums
- 8 Regal Geraniums
- 3 Edging Lobelias
- 3 Verbenas

AFTERCARE

Beautiful, blooming windowbox plants need plenty of nutrients to perform at peak levels. In addition to the granular fertilizer mixed in at planting, you should spray the flowers with a balanced, general liquid fertilizer every two weeks.

A thriving windowbox will produce many flowers. Some of these flowers, including the Miniature Roses, Nicotianas, Zinnias, Salvias, and Marigolds, make excellent cut flowers for indoor displays. Enjoy the blooms in vases and keep plants blooming by regularly deadheading your sunny windowbox flowers.

Planting a
Scented Hanging Basket

Delight your senses with fragrant flowers and lush, scented foliage in a hanging basket garden.

PLANTING YOUR SCENTED BASKET

YOU WILL NEED:

- ❏ 18 in. wire basket
- ❏ Bag of sphagnum moss
- ❏ Potting soil
- ❏ Granular fertilizer
- ❏ Polymer crystals
- ❏ Scented plants

THE PLANTS:

- ❏ 1 Dwarf English Lavender
- ❏ 1 Lemon-scented Geranium
- ❏ 1 Catmint
- ❏ 6 Sweet Peas 'Knee-Hi'
- ❏ 8 Sweet Alyssum
- ❏ 5 Dianthus 'Telstar'

1 **Line the basket** with wet sphagnum moss and fill with a mix of potting soil and slow-release fertilizer granules according to rate on package.

2 **Mix in polymer crystals** that will expand with water and help keep soil moist. Plant Sweet Alyssum around sides, inserting roots through wire.

3 **Plant upright** Lavender and the Lemon-scented Geranium in center of basket, leaving space in between and around them for fillers.

4 **At one side** of the wire basket, plant Catmint to cascade over the edges of the container. Add Sweet Peas spaced evenly around the rim.

5 **Fill in your scented** basket with Dianthus, planting it among the upright plants in the center and along the rim between other plants.

6 **Wet all sides** of basket with gentle water spray. Feed with diluted liquid fertilizer and let sit. After it drains, attach wires and hang.

Troubleshooter

For carefree watering, set up a spray mister above your basket. The mister will provide a gentle, thorough watering. They are available at most garden centers.

Tip

Hang your basket near a doorway, on a front porch, or other well-traveled area where the fragrant flowers and foliage will be brushed regularly. This will release the mixed scents.

Fragrant Eye-catcher

Mix stunning colors and enchanting perfumes for an unforgettable basket that is perfect for high-traffic areas.

INSIDE YOUR BASKET

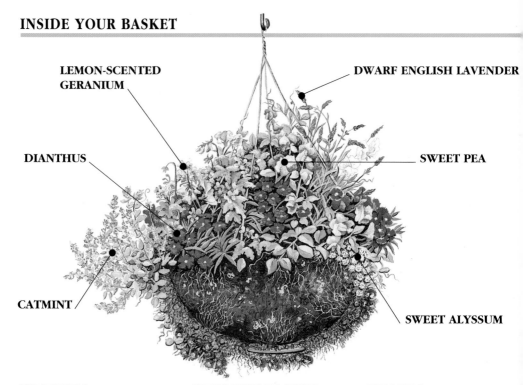

LEMON-SCENTED GERANIUM

DWARF ENGLISH LAVENDER

DIANTHUS

SWEET PEA

CATMINT

SWEET ALYSSUM

TRAILERS

- **Catmint** *(above)* has gray-green leaves with a light, spearmint fragrance. In early summer, the full foliage is covered with purple flowers.
- **Sweet Alyssum,** available in purple, white, pink, or cream, begins releasing its sweet scent in the early spring and lasts all summer.

UPRIGHT PLANTS

- **Lemon-scented Geraniums** *(above)* feature pink blooms with purple veins, and foliage that emits a citrus scent when brushed.
- **Dwarf English Lavender** bears scented, gray-green foliage and rich violet flower spikes. It provides a dramatic upright accent to the basket.

FILLERS

- **Sweet Peas** *(above)* offer early spring flowers in bright pink, purple, or white. 'Knee-Hi' is a low-growing Sweet Pea with a subtle scent.
- **Dianthus,** an old-fashioned favorite, is prized for its long bloom time and spicy, sweet fragrance. 'Telstar' offers red, white, pink, or violet blooms.

Alternative Planting Ideas

FLAVORFUL AROMA

Excite the nose and palate with a crowd of full-flavored herbs planted in a hanging basket. Hang it right outside your kitchen doorway for quick and easy access when cooking your meals.

- 2 Lime Thyme plants
- 1 Pineapple Sage
- 1 Rosemary 'Huntington Carpet'
- 1 Ornamental Onion
- 2 Society Garlics 'Silver Lace'

MIXED SCENTS

This interesting basket features a host of intriguing and complementary scented plants. The smells range from the spicy-sweet aroma of Mint, to the more subtle fragrance of Stock.

- 3 Stocks 'Trysomic 7 Weeks Mix'
- 1 Silver Thyme
- 1 Garden Phlox
- 1 Golden Apple Mint

BLOOMING BOUQUET

The refreshing smells that come from this basket are second only to the wonderful colors of the flowers. Cut the flowers as they fade to prolong the blooms.

- 2 Carnations 'Lilipot Mix'
- 8 Dianthus 'Wee Willie'
- 2 Spearmint plants
- 1 Heliotropium 'Black Beauty'
- 1 Variegated Lime-scented Geranium

AFTERCARE

Because hanging baskets need constant watering, essential nutrients may leach out too easily or quickly. To help your plants stay healthy and bloom their best, give them supplemental feedings with a general liquid fertilizer twice a month during peak bloom and growth times.

Water both the foliage and the peat moss sides of your hanging basket.

Keep your plants looking good and blooming well by trimming faded flowers and foliage. Snip the blossoms and remove some of the leaves to make a simple but colorful potpourri.

Planting a
Barrel of Bulbs

*Unbelievably bright colors
combine with classic style in
this salute to spring.*

A Floral Fantasy for Spring

Familiar, favorite flowers are accented to perfection in this collection of striking, early-blooming bulbs.

INSIDE YOUR BARREL

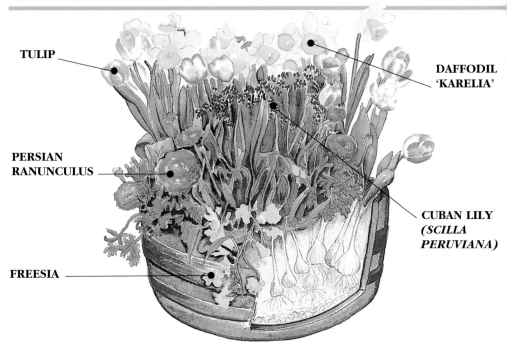

TULIP

DAFFODIL 'KARELIA'

PERSIAN RANUNCULUS

CUBAN LILY (*SCILLA PERUVIANA*)

FREESIA

UPRIGHT PLANTS

- *Tulips* (*above*) offer classic good looks. The pink, perfect blooms of these Hybrid Tulips are held aloft on sturdy stems.
- *Daffodils* are outstanding with their bold, bright flowers. 'Karelia' features big, yellow trumpets and white petals on 15 in. stems.

SPREADER

- *Cuban Lilies* (*above*) offer attractive clusters with scores of violet-blue, star-shaped blossoms that seem to sparkle with brilliant color. The cool tones and texture of these impressive flowers provide a wonderful contrast to the rich blossoms of Daffodils and Tulips.

FILLERS

- *Persian Ranunculus* (*above*) display perfectly shaped, long-lasting flowers that open to reveal rings of fine petals in bright hues.
- *Freesias* lend a sunny accent with clusters of fragrant flowers. Single or double varieties are availabl in a rainbow of colors.

PLANTING YOUR BARREL

YOU WILL NEED:

- ❏ Large oak barrel
- ❏ Drill and bit
- ❏ Landscape fabric
- ❏ Potting soil
- ❏ Bulb fertilizer
- ❏ Lightweight mulch (peat moss, compost, or cocoa hulls)

THE PLANTS:

- ❏ 14 Daffodils 'Karelia'
- ❏ 14 pink Tulips
- ❏ 2 Cuban Lilies
- ❏ 8 Freesias
- ❏ 8 Persian Ranunculus

Tip

Because these spring bloomers are planted early —fall in milder climates, early spring in cooler climates—they may need a bit of protection. Placing them near a south- or west-facing wall will help block drying winds and provide extra warmth against freezing weather. While the Daffodils and Tulips can handle light frosts, the other bulbs may be killed by a frost.

1 **Select a barrel** at least 10 in. deep. The wider the container, the more bulbs you can use. Drill several drainage holes in the bottom.

2 **Cut a circular piece** of landscape (weed-block) fabric and fit into bottom. Add 2 in. of potting soil mixed with special bulb fertilizer.

3 **Plant deep bulbs** first, massing Daffodils in rear center, surrounded on each side by groups of seven Tulips. Cover to a depth of about 5 in.

4 **Plant medium-depth** bulbs next. Place Cuban Lilies in center of barrel, and group the Freesias near the center of the front rim.

5 **Cover bulbs** with potting soil to 2 in. below rim and plant Ranunculus just beneath surface, pronged ends down, on either side of Freesias.

6 **Cover Ranunculus,** gently pat down soil, and water thoroughly. Mulch with light material such as compost, cocoa hulls, or peat moss.

Alternative Planting Ideas

WINTER SPLENDOR

Though normally associated with summer scenes, some Begonias offer bold color from fall to early spring in mild climates. These semi-tuberous Begonias offer classic, succulent leaves and profuse blooms that can be found in a wide variety of intense colors.

- 4 Rieger Begonias 'Angela'

FORCING POT

Do not limit your enjoyment of bulbs to outdoor displays. Create an artificial winter for bulbs by chilling, and then bring to a warm place to bud and bloom. These Hyacinths, Tulips, Freesias, and others illustrate the arresting results.

- 3 pink Hyacinths
- 4 Tulips
- 4 Freesias
- 2 Paperwhite Narcissus
- 4 Lily-of-the-valleys

AFTERCARE

Place your barrel in a sunny, prominent location where you can enjoy the blooms. You may need to stake taller plants to prevent flowers from falling over. Use plastic-coated wire stakes and rings. Or, gently tie stems to small bamboo sticks.

Heavy spring rains may beat down plants in full flower. Protect the display by covering the container with a simple wood and plastic tent made of rot-resistant redwood or cedar covered with clear or opaque plastic. Remove as soon as the rains stop.

ARTFUL ARRAY

Bulbs prove to be ideal candidates for portable container gardens that can be brought to center stage for dazzling displays. Here, a medley of Daffodils and pink Tulips arch over the brilliant violet flower clusters of small Grape Hyacinths.

- 18 mixed Daffodils
- 4 pink Tulips
- 16 Grape Hyacinths

Planting an
Unusual Container

Let your imagination run wild to create a fabulous flowering design in an unexpected place.

PLANTING YOUR UNUSUAL CONTAINER

YOU WILL NEED:

- ❏ 20 in. galvanized steel tub
- ❏ Window screen
- ❏ Gravel
- ❏ Sphagnum moss
- ❏ Potting soil
- ❏ Container plants

THE PLANTS:

- ❏ 3 Snapdragons
- ❏ 3 Iceland Poppies
- ❏ 1 Candytuft
- ❏ 6 Primroses 'Pacific Giants'
- ❏ 3 Ornamental Kales
- ❏ 6 Pansies
- ❏ 6 Sweet Alyssum

1 **Prepare the tub** by creating several drainage holes about 6 in. apart on the bottom of the tub. Make the holes with a nail and hammer.

2 **Ensure proper** drainage by placing a circle of window screen on the bottom. Cover with gravel and fill with soil up to an inch from the rim.

3 **Plant tall flowers** first. Set the Snapdragons in a triangle about 2-3 in. from each other. Plant the Poppies the same way. Firm soil down.

Troubleshooter

Thoroughly clean a container prior to planting. This helps to eliminate the risk of contaminating your new plants with a disease.

Tip

Water seeping from drainage holes of tubs can leave rust or water stains on concrete or wood. Put a tray under your unusual container, or move it to a surface that will not suffer water damage, such as brick, stone, or the ground.

4 **Add Candytuft** 2-3 in. to the side of the center group. Plant the Primroses, spaced uniformly, in a circle around the center group.

5 **Plant the Kale** at equal points around the edge of the tub. Fill in with Pansies and Alyssum spaced evenly around edge. Tamp all soil down.

6 **Water the container** well and place sphagnum moss around all of the plants in the tub. Position the tub in full sun, sheltered from wind.

A Novel Approach

No matter what you decide to plant in, make sure your plants relate well to each other and suit the size and style of the container.

INSIDE YOUR TUB

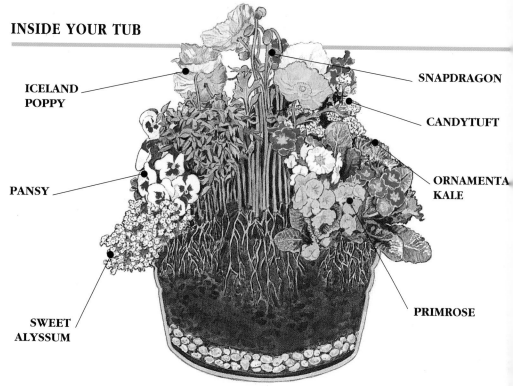

ICELAND POPPY

SNAPDRAGON

CANDYTUFT

ORNAMENTAL KALE

PANSY

PRIMROSE

SWEET ALYSSUM

FILLERS

● **Pansies** *(above)* come in stunning colors, such as the purple, orange and icy white of the 'Imperial Series'.
● **Ornamental Kale** adds unique texture with foliage in green, cream, or purple.
● **Primroses** are prized for their electric blooms, like those of 'Pacific Giants'.

TRAILERS

● **Candytuft** *(above)* grows about a foot high with a mass of lacy white, red, or pink flowers that look impressive against its dark green foliage.
● **Sweet Alyssum** is a fragrant trailing plant bearing dainty clusters of white blooms. Its cascading blooms are ideal for softening the tub's hard edges.

UPRIGHT PLANTS

● **Snapdragons** *(above)* bear clusters of tiny flowers that accent the soothing hues and tall lines of the Poppies.
● **Iceland Poppies** are true centerpieces for any container. Carried on slender 2 ft. stems, their papery blooms come in a host of dusty, warm shades.

Alternative Planting Ideas

BLOOMS IN A CASK

After they are through holding fine wine, small sherry casks can be used in the garden. Several planks have been cut out of this cask to allow for a simple, but colorful, spring garden. Wine casks are available at wineries and antique shops.

- 3 Daffodils
- 3 purple Primroses
- 3 red Primroses

DRY WEATHER POT

For a truly unusual container, include uncommon plants. This formed concrete container makes a unique addition to a patio or deck, and the succulents used in this planting can thrive with very little moisture. Many nurseries and specialty shops sell concrete pots.

- 4 Snowball Cacti
- 4 Golden Ball Cacti
- 4 *Pachycereus pringlei*

GARDEN ON WHEELS

An old-fashioned wheelbarrow provides a country look and offers enough space to plant a small bed of flowers. Use simple, solid bloom colors to complement the sturdy frame of the wheelbarrow. Browse antique stores and local auction houses for refurbished wooden wheelbarrows.

- 14 red Geraniums
- 6 blue Lobelias

AFTERCARE

If you are using a metal container, check its bottom for rust after the first year. If you find rust, sand down and paint your container before planting in it again.

Water every rainless day because container plants dry out more rapidly than plants grown in the ground. Use a watering "wand", available at garden centers. The wand emits a gentle stream of water that will not damage delicate flower stems.

Remove flowers as soon as the blooms begin to fade and you will usually be rewarded with another set of blooms in your container.

TASKS & TECHNIQUES

A Basic Guide to
Choosing Container Plants

A variety of container plants in many sizes and price ranges gives you creative options.

Easy to Buy, Move, and Transplant

Variety and ease of care make container plants a smart choice.

WHY BUY CONTAINER PLANTS?

Most plants are available in containers, with a wide variety of plant types, sizes, and prices suitable for every garden need. Container plants are available in all seasons and allow you to choose the exact bloom or leaf color you want. They are easy to transplant and need not be planted immediately. You can pay more for large landscape plants for instant impact, or go with smaller, less expensive choices.

WHEN TO BUY

It is best to buy plants early in the growing season so you can get them into the

Container plants are available in a variety of sizes

Tip

Do not buy container plants that are overgrown and badly rootbound; they have lived in their containers too long and will not thrive. Recognize such plants by the thick roots growing out of bottom of containers; they may have roots coming up out of soil surface as well.

garden as soon as possible. Plants left in containers can be held for a long time with no adverse effects as long as you keep them out of bright, hot sun and do not allow their roots to dry out.

Before buying, look at plants in the season they put on a show to see their key features—such as flowers, fruit, or fall color. Plants that are not yet in bloom will establish more quickly, but you may wish to purchase one with buds or a few open blooms to verify color.

HOW TO CHOOSE

Look for overall good health and vigor with fresh, lush foliage, sturdy stems and branches, lots of flower buds, and deep color. Well-cared for nursery stock will show good growth, the result of adequate and consistent watering and fertilizing.

Check the root system by feeling under the soil for circling, tangled roots. Look at the bottom to see if roots protrude. Have a nursery professional pull plant from pot to inspect rootball if you feel it may be rootbound.

Small plants including annuals and vegetables should be compact (not leggy) with fresh foliage and abundant buds or leaves.

Inspect leaves to check heal

EVALUATING CONTAINER PLANTS: FOUR WAYS

When choosing trees, look for sturdy trunks. Trees should stand upright without the nursery stake (even though they should be staked when planted to speed the development of a sturdy root system that can withstand winds). Roots should be able to support top; tree should not look like a bareroot plant that was potted up the previous week. To check the sturdiness of trunk and roots, ask a nursery professional to remove the stake.

Look at the overall plant. Consider size: it should not look top-heavy or seem too big for its container. Smaller plants adapt better in garden.

Invert pot and look for roots growing through the drainage holes. A few small roots are not a problem, but many or large roots could be.

Evaluate branch structure. Plants should appear well-proportioned, not leggy or lopsided with uneven or sparse growth patterns.

Check foliage and flower buds. Leaves should look fresh and show a healthy color. Flower buds should be plump and numerous.

EVALUATING CONTAINER PLANTS: THREE TIPS

Avoid plants that show yellowed or blemished leaves. They are lacking key nutrients and will have difficulty growing well after transplanting.

Do not purchase plants with chewed, ragged leaves—the result of insect damage. Plants will not thrive, and bugs could spread in your garden.

Avoid plants with dead stems or leaves. Both could be a sign of disease, dieback, or too much or too little water; such plants may not grow well.

Common Types of Container Plants

	TYPE	DESCRIPTION
	Boxed tree *(left)*	Large landscape trees several years old; difficult to move and plant but offer instant impact on landscape; quick to mature; expensive; limited availability; may need to be ordered
	15 gallon	Many trees and shrubs available in this size; large yet still moveable, three- to five-year-old plants; requires large planting hole; cost varies but substantially cheaper than
	5 gallon *(left)*	Common size for many trees, shrubs, vines, and some perennials; good-sized plants; easy to lift and transport; requires no difficult digging for planting; slightly more costly
	1 gallon	Most trees, shrubs, perennials, herbs, vegetables, annuals, groundcovers, vines, and succulents available in this size; easy to plant; many varieties fill in quickly; less expensive
	4 inch *(left)*	Good choice for perennials, herbs, vegetables, annuals, and groundcovers where you want many plants for quick cover; easy to transport and plant in large quantities; inexpensive
	Six-pack	Good choice for annuals, vegetables, and fast-growing herbs or perennials; plants start small but establish quickly and may catch up in size to 4 inch or gallon plants; very economical
	Flat *(left)*	Common for groundcovers and some annuals and hedge plants where you need many of the same kind of plant; small plants are easy to plant; best value per square inch

Seasonal Tips

SPRING
Choosing plants
Select from a huge variety of available plants from local nurseries or garden centers as weather warms and planting season begins. Spring is the perfect time to start vegetable gardens or new flower gardens using economical six-packs or 4 in. pots.

FALL
Selecting foliage plants
Fall foliage plants will be at their peak so purchase plants now if you want this feature, especially if trying to match the color in multiple plantings. In mild climates, fall is a good time to purchase and plant permanent landscape plants such as trees, shrubs, vines, perennials, and groundcovers.

WINTER
Protecting
Cover new transplants with a layer of loose mulch to help them through the first winter.

Weather Watch

If warm spells hit, delay transplanting until weather cools to minimize stress. Keep plants shaded; water daily to keep roots moist.

A Guide to Container
Selection and Care

Choosing the right container for your plants promotes good health and good-looking displays.

Picking the Perfect Planter

Chosen with care, an attractive container plant steals the show.

WHAT TO CHOOSE

Container choices offer almost limitless possibilities. Traditional clay pots range in size from 2 in. to over 2 ft. high and wide, while wooden containers include spacious half-whiskey barrels that can house trees.

Prices range from very inexpensive plastic pots to pricey, ornate, glazed ceramic bowls. Even the range of styles is wide—from practical paper pulp pots to formal designs in wood, faux-stone, or fiberglass copies of terra-cotta urns. Almost any container with good drainage will work as a planter.

HOW TO CHOOSE

The most striking container gardens blend well with their

Use containers of different sizes to frame an entryway

site and meet the growing needs of the plants.

Ideally, your container should complement its surroundings. A formal entry may call for a Victorian urn, while a rustic box may look good in a country garden. Clay pots work well on brick patios, and wooden planters are suited to decks.

For the healthiest container plantings, choose containers that provide enough space for the plant's roots. Slow-growing plants, such as conifers, need pots only slightly larger than their rootball. Give fast-growing flowers and vegetables room to expand by selecting a pot equal in volume to the eventual mature size of the top growth of the plant.

Match the container to your plant's moisture needs. Moisture-loving plants dry quickly in porous clay, paper pulp, or hanging baskets. Plastic, concrete, and glazed ceramic hold moisture better. Regardless of size or type, make sure your container provides adequate drainage and drill holes as necessary.

HOW TO CARE FOR CONTAINERS

Regularly examine your containers, as well as supports for hanging basket or windowboxes, for signs of wear, and take steps to keep them in good condition. Replace cracked clay pots and any wooden containers that show signs of rot.

Heavy pots should be lifted off the ground to reduce decay and to keep them from staining the surface. Place pot "feet", ha bricks, or saucers under heavy containers.

Clean containers with a solution of water with 10 percent household bleach before replanting. Use a brush to scrub away minera stains on clay pots.

Use a masonry bit to drill

Tip

Terra-cotta pots are porous and can draw water away from the plants inside. To help plants establish, soak terra-cotta pots for an hour before planting. When watering, douse the pot as well as the plant.

CHECKLIST FOR CHOOSING CONTAINERS

Tip

Using a liner—a pot within a pot—allows you to easily replace plants that have passed their peak. In cold climates, use plastic pots as liners.

Drainage. Make sure the container has at least one hole in the bottom to provide drainage. Only bog plants will survive in pots without holes.

Depth. The container should be deep enough to allow all plant roots to grow without crowding. Use deep pots for deep-rooted plants.

Weight. If your filled container will be moved, or if you use many for a rooftop or balcony garden, be sure to choose a lightweight container.

Frostproof. Many containers will crack if temperatures drop below freezing. Ask seller if container is frostproof, or empty before frost to be safe.

Color. Dark-colored pots absorb heat; they may cook roots in hot, sunny climates, and dry out quickly. Light-colored pots tend to stay cool.

KEEPING CONTAINERS IN GOOD CONDITION

Sterilize used containers by washing with a 10 percent bleach solution. Scrub away any stains and rinse well.

Empty containers of all plant soil before cold sets in. Moisture in soil could freeze and damage containers.

Weatherize clay pots by coating the outside with marine varnish or a clear plastic coating for exterior use.

Common Plant Containers

TYPE	BENEFITS	TIPS
Clay dish or bowl	Shallow and wide for attractive, low display; good in front of other containers	Use with shallow-rooted plants; water frequently; mulch soil surface
Terra-cotta (unglazed clay) *(left)*	Huge variety of sizes and styles; inexpensive and widely available; attractive anywhere	Soak in water for one hour before using; empty or bring in before winter
Wooden planter	Natural look; complements wooden decks and siding; variety of sizes and shapes available	Needs tight-fitting sides for water retention; line with plastic
Glazed ceramic *(left)*	Ornamental; available in all colors and formal, textured, or boldly patterned styles	May need to install drain holes unless another pot with holes is set inside
Windowbox	Specific sizes and widths to fit below windows; can be painted to match trim	Good for shallow-rooted annuals; use lightweight soil; affix with brackets
Wooden tub *(left)*	Large size allows room for mature, small trees, such as citrus and dwarf varieties	Good for trees and shrubs; coat interior with non-toxic preservative
Half-barrel	Rustic look with excellent water retention; extra-large size suitable for largest container plantings	Accommodates roots of larger trees and shrubs; ideal for water garden
Concrete *(left)*	The most weather resistant and durable for all climates; holds up to some freezing temperatures	Available in wide range of sizes and styles; move to final site before planting
Faux-stone	Lightweight; offers good insulation; easily made at home using bowls or planters; ages well	Purchase ready-made, or custom-make to suit your planting needs
Paper pulp *(left)*	Inexpensive, lightweight, and allows direct transplanting into other containers or to the garden	Seldom last longer than three years, so use only for temporary plantings
Plastic	Large variety of sizes, shapes, and colors; non-porous for good water retention; lightweight and portable	Containers last longer if kept out of full sun; dark containers get hot in sun
Wire basket *(left)*	Ideal for hanging basket or wall displays; makes good focal point; many sizes and shapes	Line sides with sphagnum moss and plant entire basket; water often
Metal	Gives unique, contemporary look and feel to blend with other metal accents or sculptures	Use only cast aluminum alloy or line with plastic liners to prevent corrosion

A Guide to Making
Faux Stone Containers

These inexpensive, easy-to-make planters rival old stone troughs for good looks and versatility.

Create character and instant age-old charm using a simple recipe.

WHAT IS FAUX STONE?

Faux stone is a term that refers to a mixture of sand, peat moss or vermiculite, and cement mixed and wetted to form lightweight containers that resemble old-fashioned stone sinks or troughs.

WHY USE IT?

It is inexpensive, easy, and rewarding to construct your own containers using this method, especially since real stone containers are both expensive and difficult to find. These homemade planters are lightweight, long-lasting, and attractive. They are the perfect vehicle to show off a collection of alpines or other small plants.

Use different molds to make a variety of sizes and shapes

Tip

An alternative to using cardboard box forms is to use two plastic containers such as windowboxes or even storage boxes. Just be sure the difference between the two containers is 2 in. on all sides so the new trough will have thick walls.

HOW TO MAKE FAUX STONE CONTAINERS

Start with equal parts of coarse sand and cement to two parts peat moss. Thoroughly mix these dry ingredients and then slowly add enough water to the mix until everything is moist. Continue adding water until you have a fairly stiff mixture that will hold together.

Create the container by packing mixture in bottom and in gaps between two forms, which usually consist of an inner and outer box or dish. The outer form should be 2 in. wider and longer than the inner. This allows a gap large enough for the material to form thick, strong sides that approximate the dimensions of old stone sinks or troughs. Or, use the mix to coat your existing, large

clay pots for attractive, instantly aged containers.

After a few days, when firm enough to pick up but not yet rock-hard, carefully remove the forms. Use a wir▌ brush to gently round off corners or bring out texture▌ Let empty dishes and trough▌ dry or "cure" for a few wee▌ to strengthen them.

Dishes are easy to make

MAKING A FAUX STONE TROUGH

YOU WILL NEED:

- ❏ I bag Portland cement
- ❏ I bag coarse sand
- ❏ Peat moss or vermiculite
- ❏ Bucket of water
- ❏ Wheelbarrow
- ❏ Chicken wire
- ❏ Cardboard box, 12 in. long by 10 in. wide
- ❏ Cardboard box, 14 in. long by 12 in. wide
- ❏ Trowel
- ❏ Wooden dowel or stick
- ❏ Knife
- ❏ Spray mister

1 **Mix together** one part cement, one part sand, and two parts peat moss (or vermiculite) in a wheelbarrow until it looks well blended.

2 **Add water** slowly to make a stiff mixture that just holds together in your hand. Mix thoroughly to coat and moisten all ingredients.

Tip

Create a faux stone pot by soaking an ordinary clay pot in water and coating it with a layer of the cement-sand-peat moss mixture. Wearing gloves, coat sides and rim. Coat a few inches down inside to hide the clay pot underneath.

3 **Cut a piece** of chicken wire to fit around inner box. Form it around outside of box to act as a reinforcement to strengthen the forms.

4 **Trowel 2-3 in.** of mix into bottom of larger box. Place wire-covered box inside. Use a stick to pack mix around sides and eliminate air pockets.

Tip

For a different look, use vermiculite instead of peat moss. This will change the color and texture of your container slightly for a nice variation, yet the material offers equal strength.

5 **After two weeks,** pull away inner box and check if mix is hard and dry. Gently fold box inward and lift out slowly to avoid damaging sides.

6 **Once hardened,** cut and peel away outer box. Try not to damage the walls. Spray stubborn pieces with water and peel away with a knife.

Seasonal Tips

AFTERCARE

Use a wire brush along any edges of the trough that appear too smooth. This roughens the surface, exposing the gritty sand to create a more attractive, aged, textured look. Do this carefully to avoid crumbling away excess amounts from the sides, especially if container has not completely hardened.

EARLY SPRING
Planning
Create your container several weeks before spring planting to ensure maximum longevity. This allows plenty of time for it to dry or "cure". Plus, you get to enjoy the container the first season (rather than having to wait a year).

SUMMER
Assembling & Planting
Make faux stone containers in dry summer weather, when the ingredients will dry rapidly. Choose late-blooming types of plants to enjoy the show in the coming months of fall. Use small-scale plants, both upright and trailing varieties, to fill your planter *(above)*.

Weather Watch

During prolonged periods of summer heat, be sure to check any newly planted faux stone containers frequently for soil moisture. Small planters can dry out very quickly in warm weather. The young plants need consistent moisture levels to form healthy roots and establish quickly.

Before you plant the trough, you will need to drill drain holes in the bottom. Invert container, support it well, and—using a high speed drill with masonry bits—slowly begin drilling holes. Do not force the bit as you may crack the bottom. Drill several holes in various places.

A Basic Guide to
Repotting Plants

Keep your container plants in top form by giving their roots fresh soil and room to grow.

REPOTTING: REUSING THE SAME CONTAINER

YOU WILL NEED:

- ❑ Potted plant
- ❑ Blunt knife
- ❑ Pruning shears
- ❑ Broken pot shards
- ❑ Potting soil
- ❑ Watering can

Tip

For an extra measure of success, thoroughly scrub out the old container with detergent before you repot. Remove any crust around pot rim, leftover soil, and roots. You may want to use a 10 percent bleach solution to sterilize the container.

1 **Inspect plant** to see if it is potbound or roots are growing out of the drain hole. Check if pot is in good enough shape to reuse. Water well.

2 **After an hour,** tilt pot on its side and pull plant free, holding main stem as you gently tug. Run a knife along the sides to free stuck roots.

3 **Loosen roots,** especially those growing in a circle around bottom. Prune off broken roots and cut back the longest roots by about a third.

4 **Cover drainage hole** with pot shards, add soil, and replace plant. Center and level plant. Backfill and firm the soil with fingers. Water well.

REPOTTING: MOVING TO A LARGER CONTAINER

YOU WILL NEED: ❑ Container plant ❑ Pruning shears ❑ Larger pot ❑ Potting soil

1 **With the pot on** its side, gently tap container against a hard surface to loosen soil before you slide out rootball.

2 **Gently pull apart** the roots. Trim off broken roots and cut back any overly long roots by about a third.

3 **In a pot 2 in. larger** in diameter, replant using fresh soil mix in bottom and around the sides. Water well.

Giving Potted Plants a New Start

To ensure long-term health, use containers that suit the plant.

WHY REPOT?

Transferring a plant to a bigger pot, or refreshing the soil in the same pot, is necessary for continued health and vigor for nearly all container plants, including bulbs, perennials, shrubs, trees, and water plants.

WHEN TO REPOT

Cramped, tangled roots, stunted growth, few flowers, or an excess need for water are signs that a plant is in need of repotting. An older plant doing poorly may have pot-bound, massed roots in need of trimming, space, and fresh soil. A large, young plant whose roots are coming out of the drain hole is ready for a larger pot.

The best time to repot a plant is when stress will be at a minimum, either prior to new growth in spring, after it has finished active growth and flowering, or when dormant. Repot deciduous plants after their leaves drop; repot evergreens in late fall or early spring. For flowering plants, repot a season or two before flowering or after the blooms fade.

Healthy roots mean healthy container plants

HOW TO REPOT

Remove the plant carefully by tilting the container and gently tugging on the main stems as you support the foliage. If no movement occurs, slide a knife down the sides to loosen the roots.

Gently tease apart tight roots, removing soil as you work. Prune back fibrous roots by about one third.

Repot in a larger container (usually 2-3 in. wider) for young plants that need space to mature. If using a clay container, soak the pot overnight to reduce stress on the plant. If your plant has reached a mature size, repot in the same container adding fresh soil.

Add fresh, lightweight, sterile soil mix in the bottom of the pot. Position the plant in the center and spread out the roots. Add more soil around the sides, gently working it in between the roots and firming with your fingers. Water well and keep plants shaded for a week.

Tip

Instead of repotting, you can refresh container plants yearly by removing the top 2-4 in. of soil and replacing with fresh soil mix. Avoid damaging the tender feeder roots near soil surface.

Soak clay pots before using

Seasonal Tips

AFTERCARE

During the repotting process, some stems may become broken or damaged. Prune away these stems, cutting just above a leaf bud so that you do not leave any dead wood. Prune lightly as needed to shape the plant.

Once you see signs of new growth, you know the plant is on its way to renewed vigor. Feed it using a weak solution of liquid fertilizer every two to three weeks, especially before flowering. Too frequent or too strong a fertilization program will lead to an abundance of growth, especially on permanent plants, which will mean early repotting.

FALL
Repotting
In warm winter areas, repot deciduous plants in fall after their leaves drop *(above)*. (Wait until spring in cold winter areas.) This reduces stress and allows the roots to settle and heal over the winter for good growth in early spring. Repot spring-blooming shrubs and bulbs, conifers, and perennials.

SPRING
Transferring
Transfer young plants to larger containers in early spring before the rush of new growth. After last frost date, repot summer- and fall-flowering plants, summer-flowering bulbs, conifers, perennials, and annuals.

Weather Watch

Reduce stress on newly repotted plants when warm weather hits by giving them ample water and plenty of shade. Move them to a shady spot, or construct temporary shade using stakes and fabric. Roots must stay moist. Also keep plants out of the wind, which leads to dry soil.

PLANT GUIDE

Calla Lilies

Silk-textured funnels of bloom all summer

Season	Special Features	Best Conditions	

Flowers in summer	Easy to grow
	  Good for cutting
	 Disease resistant
		All zones
		  Full sun or partial shade
		  Moist, well-drained soil
			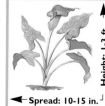
			 Height: 1-3 ft.
			 ◄ Spread: 10-15 in.

Exotic Trumpet Blooms

Shapely and elegant Calla Lilies bring a touch of tropical color to any garden.

COLORS & VARIETIES

Calla Lilies produce handsome, arrow-shaped leaves and waxy, upright, cup-shaped spathes (the flowers) in white, yellow, pink, salmon, or red. Hardy in zones 8-10, in colder zones Calla Lilies are planted in spring and lifted in fall for winter storage.

Classic white Calla Lilies, including the 2 ft. tall 'Black-eyed Beauty' and the 12 in. 'Godfrey', have a proper and formal look. 'Green Goddess' reaches 3 ft. and bears beautiful, green flowers with white centers.

For a more colorful effect try 'Flame', a brilliant orange-red. 'Treasure' is a glowing golden orange that will light up the landscape.

Calla Lilies also offer pastel hues. 'Cameo' is pale peach with a deep red throat, while *Zantedeschia rehmannii* is a vigorous plant with rosy pink flowers.

WHERE TO PLANT

Plant Calla Lilies anywhere you want a bold accent plant. Even when they are not in bloom, the glossy foliage is always an asset.

Taller Calla Lilies are a striking accent in the center of an island flower bed, where their presence will ensure that the bed never looks thin or insubstantial.

A few clumps of medium-tall Calla Lilies in the middle row will unite a flower border all season, as perennials come and go.

Calla Lilies look especially natural growing near water. Plant them next to a pond or stream, where they can appreciate the extra moisture, but be sure that the soil's drainage is good.

PERFECT PARTNERS

Calla Lilies combine easily with other flowers and with foliage plants, as long as you keep the scale of their bold leaves in mind.

Fancy-leaved Caladium in shades of red and pink pair up beautifully with rose pink Calla Lily 'Dominique' or deep pink 'Galaxy'. Caladiums and Calla Lilies can be planted and lifted at the same time.

Pale yellow Calla Lilies such as 'Solfatare', look wonderful with a blue-flowered vine. Combine them with Passion Flowers, hardy in your area, or annual Morning Glories.

Rich violet 'Lavender Gem' Calla Lilies contrast well with the tousled heads of Bee Balm in shades of pink, crimson, and purple.

Calla Lilies with white Roses

The golden Z. elliottiana

Calla Lilies and Geraniums

an entryway

Near water, plant the white *Z. aethiopica* in a damp spot with Siberian Irises. The contrast of the plants' foliage and blooms will be lovely.

Bicolored 'Green Goddess'

PLANTING & AFTERCARE

YOU WILL NEED: ❏ Calla Lily rhizomes ❏ Fork ❏ Compost ❏ Mulch ❏ Balanced (20-20-20) fertilizer

1 **Plant in spring** when temperatures stay above 40 degrees F. Fork over the area to loosen soil to a depth of 8 in., adding compost.

2 **Dig a 3 in. deep hole** for each rhizome, spacing holes 8-12 in. apart. Set horizontally in the holes, growing eyes pointed up.

3 **Cover with soil** and firm gently. Water and add a thick layer of mulch. In colder zones, wait for soil to warm before mulching.

4 **Keep plants** well watered during growing season. Fertilize monthly. Cut off faded flowers to help the plants bloom longer.

5 **In regions** colder than zone 8, dig up rhizomes before frost. Dry a few days, clean off dead leaves and soil, and store in a cool, dry place.

Dollar Sense

To increase your stock of Callas, cut rhizomes into several pieces in spring, making sure each section has a growing eye.

Secrets of Success

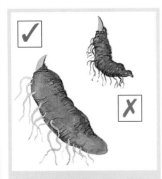

BUYING HINTS

- **Buy the largest** rhizomes you can find. When you squeeze them, they should feel firm and plump.
- **Avoid soft, limp, or dry** rhizomes. Do not buy small rhizomes, as they may only produce leaves in their first year of growth.

SUN & SOIL

- **Full sun to partial** shade. In hot climates, Calla Lilies will do best with some shade. Further north, they can take full sun.
- **Well-drained soil.** Calla Lilies need plenty of water, but will rot in soil that is constantly wet.

SPECIAL ADVICE

- **The refrigerator** provides the perfect storage area for dormant Calla Lilies. Keep rhizomes in a paper bag, away from fruits.
- **For earlier blooms,** start Calla Lilies in small pots indoors in late winter. Plant out when frost has passed.

Seasonal Tips

SPRING
Planting
Plant rhizomes outdoors when night temperatures remain above 40 degrees F. Or, set out started plants after the last spring frost.

SUMMER
Fertilizing & Deadheading
Water, fertilize, and deadhead Calla Lilies (*right*) regularly to keep your plants at their best all summer.

EARLY FALL
Lifting & Storing
Before first frost, dig up and dry off rhizomes. Store in a dry, cool place over winter. Or, let the rhizomes rest for a month, then pot them for indoor winter color.

Plant Doctor

Dry rot can attack stored Calla Lily rhizomes. Discard dry and crumbly rhizomes and soak the rest in a mild fungicide for six hours as a preventive measure.

Catmints

A haze of blue flowers hovers over aromatic foliage

Season	Special Features	Best Conditions	
P Perennial	🌵 Drought resistant	🌐 Zones 3-11	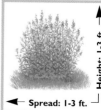
✳ Flowers in summer	🕷 Disease resistant	☀ Full sun	Height: 1-3 ft.
	≋ Good groundcover	🔨 Well-drained soil	Spread: 1-3 ft.

Mounds of Textured Foliage

The lavender-blue blossoms and gray leaves of Catmints lend cool hues to the summer garden.

COLORS & VARIETIES

Above mounds of softly textured foliage, Catmints *(Nepeta)* send up many spikes of tubular, 1/2-1 in. long flowers. Although most Catmints bloom in shades of lavender and blue, there are varieties with white and yellow flowers.

Common Catmint *(Nepeta x faassenii)* grows 18 in. tall and about 24 in. wide, with many 1/2 in. long, lavender-blue flowers and scented, gray leaves. The 'Blue Dwarf' cultivar is more compact, to 12 in. tall, with pale blue flowers.

Siberian Catmint *(N. sibirica)* is an upright, 2-3 ft. tall plant. It blooms for many months with a show of 1 in. long, purplish blue flowers.

The unusually colored 'Snowflake' bears lovely, creamy white flowers on a mounding plant that reaches a mere 1-1 1/2 ft. in height.

'Dropmore' edges a walkway

Impressive 'Six Hills Giant'

WHERE TO PLANT

Plant Catmints where you can enjoy both their aromatic foliage and delightful flowers. Catmints are ideal for groundcovers, as edging plants, and in herb gardens or perennial borders.

For a colorful groundcover in full sun, plant low-growing varieties. They will quickly spread and carpet the ground in a profusion of delicate blooms.

Low-growing varieties are also well suited as edging plants. Plant them along a walkway where their softly scented foliage will be appreciated by a passersby.

No herb garden is complete without at least one variety of Catmint. In addition to adding color to the garden, the plant's leaves can be used in tea.

PERFECT PARTNERS

The soft mounds of gray foliage and cool flower colors of Catmints are best

Catmints and Dianthus 'Prin⟨

used to help soften or blend bold-colored plants.

Plant drifts of tall, dark violet-blooming 'Six Hills Giant' Catmints between pink-blooming 'Carefree Wonder' Roses to softly link Rose bushes to one another

The 18 in. 'Blue Beauty creates a perfect middle ground between tall, white

Catmints and gold Columbin⟨

'Salmon' edging a lawn

Miss Lingard' Phlox and low-
growing, white-flowered
Snow-in-summer. Its large,
blue blooms intensify the
white of the other plants.

For a vibrant and long-
lasting border, interplant
'Blue Wonder' Catmints with
yellow 'Moonshine' Yarrow.
The complementary colors
will radiate their deep hues.

diate with color

PLANTING & AFTERCARE

YOU WILL NEED: ❏ Catmint plants in gallon
containers ❏ Shovel ❏ Compost

1 **Plant Catmints** in early
fall or after last frost in
spring. For each plant, dig a
hole several inches deeper
and wider than the container.

2 **Add a shovelful** of
compost to each hole,
working it into the soil.
Remove plant from container
by gently inverting it.

3 **If roots are matted,**
gently loosen them with
your fingers. Place plant in
hole so the crown is a little
higher than surrounding soil.

4 **Firm soil around** the
rootball. Water with a
hose, soaking the planting
area. Water again when top
inch of soil is dry.

Dollar Sense

Catmints are easy to
propagate from tip cuttings
made in late spring. Cut
4 in. long pieces from tips
of stems. Remove leaves
from bottom 2 in. Insert
1 in. apart in an equal mix
of vermiculite and perlite,
or in sand. Place in a
shaded but well-lit spot,
and water when mix is dry.

Secrets of Success

BUYING HINTS

- **Buy plants** in spring or early fall in large containers. Choose Catmint plants with vigorous stems and leaves.
- **Avoid plants with** wilted or yellowed leaves. Do not buy plants with roots protruding from the drainage holes.

SUN & SOIL

- **Full sun.** Catmints bloom best in full sun. They tolerate heat, but do not grow well in high humidity.
- **Well-drained soil.** Heavy clay soils may cause the roots and stems of Catmints to rot, especially during the winter months.

SPECIAL ADVICE

- **The species forms** of Catmints can be raised from seeds sown in fall directly in the garden.
- **Catmint appeals** to some cats. If you do not want cats in your yard, plant Kashmir Catmint (*N. govaniana*). It does not attract them.

Seasonal Tips

EARLY SPRING
Cutting back
As new growth begins, cut out all old dead stems at the base with pruning shears.

SPRING
Dividing
Divide Catmints every two to three years to rejuvenate the plants and obtain more plants. With a shovel, dig up plants and divide. Replant in soil prepared with compost.

SUMMER
Shearing
Just after blooming, shear

Catmints back halfway to remove dead flower spikes and keep the plants more compact (*below*). They will often rebloom later in summer or in early fall.

Plant Doctor

Catmints are seldom bothered by insects or diseases. However, cats can seriously damage some types by rolling on them, crushing the stems and leaves. Try placing thorny twigs among the stems to help protect the plants.

Chrysanthemums

Abundant flowers for a brilliant fall finale

Season	*Special Features*	*Best Conditions*	
Perennial	Fast growing	Zones 5-10	
Flowers in fall	Good for cutting	Full sun	Height: 10-36 in.
		Rich, well-drained soil	◄—Spread: 18-20 in.

Carefree Autumn Color

Plant Chrysanthemums to bring bright, beautiful colors to the late season garden.

COLORS & VARIETIES

Garden Chrysanthemums *(Chrysanthemum x morifolium)* feature blooms in every color except blue. They offer a remarkable variety of both flower forms and plant habits.

Dependable, easy-to-grow selections include compact, double-flowered Cushion Mums such as claret purple 'Gypsy Wine', white 'Spotless', and bright yellow, 14 in. tall 'Sunny Morning'. Mounding Button Mums such as bronze 'Brown Eyes' and red 'Little Rascal' are also compact and reliable.

Single-flowered Mums such as 20 in. 'Daisy White' are charming with their yellow centers. Decorative, fancy-petalled Mums include varieties whose flowers have spooned, quilled, reflexed, or spider-like petals. 'Carousel' has large, silvery lilac blooms with spooned tips; rosy lilac 'Centerpiece' is quilled.

With shrubs and annuals

WHERE TO PLANT

Garden Chrysanthemums are excellent choices for flower borders, containers of all sorts, and cutting gardens.

With such a wide range of plant heights available, Chrysanthemums add variety and interest to a fall border. Select short types of Cushion or Button Mums to edge the border. Use taller, 1 ½-2 ft., single-flowered or decorative types in the middle of beds.

Mums in containers bring a deck or patio alive in autumn. Arrange plants in single pots 8-12 in. wide. Or, group them by color in larger pots or raised beds.

Chrysanthemums are an indispensable part of any cutting garden, providing armloads of fresh flowers for fall arrangements right up to the first hard frosts.

PERFECT PARTNERS

With hundreds of selections in a wide variety of colors to

'Raquel' and Prairie Dropse

choose from, versatile Chrysanthemums make exciting partners for many other fall-flowering plants.

In a perennial border, place several 12 in. tall, bronze 'Bandit' Cushion Chrysanthemums in front of 30 in., blue-flowered *Aster frikartii.* Several 5 ft. tall Maiden Grass clumps make dramatic background.

Combine pale-flowered Chrysanthemums such as white 'Chardonnay' or pink 'Chiffon'—both 18 in. tall Cushion Mums—in front of taller 'Snowbank' Boltonias and cool blue Russian Sages for a softer effect.

A planting made up of a number of Chrysanthemum in complementary autumnal

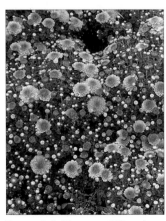

Rose pink blooms of 'Lynn'

autumn

colors will be attractive for weeks. Try combining short varieties such as bronze 'Hopscotch' and creamy 'Valour' with taller, tawny gold 'Best Regards' and clear yellow 'Classic'.

Spooned 'Yellow Illusion'

PLANTING & AFTERCARE

YOU WILL NEED: ❏ Mum plants ❏ Hoe ❏ Garden fork ❏ Compost ❏ Fertilizer ❏ Trowel ❏ Mulch

1 Plant Mums after last frost. For best results, prepare bed a few weeks before planting time. Remove weeds and rocks from area.

2 Mix in a 3 in. layer of compost or well-rotted manure. Work in a complete fertilizer, following directions on label. Water if soil is dry.

3 With a trowel, dig a planting hole for each Mum, spacing plants 16-18 in. apart. Place each plant in its hole, spreading roots gently.

4 Firm soil around roots. Water well. Place a thin layer of mulch such as shredded leaves around plants to conserve moisture.

Tip

To keep Chrysanthemums blooming well, divide the clumps every year or two in spring when shoots are about 5 in. tall. Dig up the entire clump and use a knife to cut divisions from the outside; discard the woody center. Replant divisions as soon as possible in well-prepared soil.

Secrets of Success

BUYING HINTS

- **Buy well-rooted,** young Chrysanthemums in spring. Choose either divisions or plants grown from cuttings.
- **Avoid plants** that are very small or have not had time to form good roots. Do not buy any plants that are harboring insects.

SUN & SOIL

- **Full sun.** Mums grow and bloom best in full sun; they become spindly in shade. In very hot areas, they prefer some light afternoon shade.
- **Rich, well-drained soil.** If soil is poorly drained, add plenty of organic matter or plant in raised beds.

SPECIAL ADVICE

- **For sturdy plants** and larger flowers, regularly pinch stems back to six or seven leaves in mid-summer to allow buds to form.
- **Taller varieties** may need staking in windy areas. Place small stakes around plants and circle with twine.

Seasonal Tips

SPRING
Propagating
Take cuttings when shoots are 3-4 in. long. Insert ends in damp sand or perlite *(below right)*. Keep in well-lit spot out of direct sun until roots form. Pot up or plant out in the garden.

SUMMER
Fertilizing & Watering
Feed Chrysanthemums twice during growing season with a complete fertilizer. Water deeply when top inch of soil is dry. Overwatering causes leaves to yellow and die; lack of water leads to woody stems that lose lower leaves.

LATE FALL
Cutting back & Mulching
Cut back spent flowering stems. In regions with cold winters, cover plants with straw and evergreen boughs after soil has frozen.

Plant Doctor

If you see silvery white streaks on the leaves and flowers of Mums, suspect either chrysanthemum or greenhouse thrips. These tiny ($1/20$-$1/16$ in.) insects hide inside leaf and flower buds. Pick off and destroy infested leaves and flowers to control.

Cyclamens

Butterfly-like blooms hover above colorful foliage

Season	*Special Features*	*Best Conditions*	
✹ Flowers in fall, winter, or spring	🌵 Drought resistant	🌐 Zones 5-10	
	⚘ Self-seeding	☀ Partial to full shade	
	⚘ Some varieties: fragrant	✎ Well-drained, neutral soil	Height: 2-8 in.
			◄ Spread: 4-12 in.

Dainty Garden Gems

The silver-marked leaves of Cyclamens are topped with bouquets of exotic blooms.

COLORS & VARIETIES

Cyclamens are sturdy enough to make a year-round home in the garden. Flowers with twisted, swept-back petals appear in fall, winter, or spring (depending on the species) in shades of pink, crimson, or white.

Ivy-leaved Cyclamen has rose-pink autumn flowers above mounds of silver-marbled foliage; it sometimes produces flowers in summer as well. It is hardy to zone 5, and can be grown further north where snow cover is reliable. 'Album' is a white-flowered selection.

Cyclamen coum is just as hardy, and available in white, pink, or red. It flowers in late winter or spring, with some intermittent blooms through the summer and into fall.

In zones 7-10, choose *C. cilicium* for fall blooms, as it does not require winter frost to remain vigorous. The pale pink blossoms have a rose-pink blotch at their bases.

The pure white 'Kaori Series'

The butterfly-like blooms

C. cyprium is only 2 in. tall, but has large, showy, white flowers marked with red at the base. Best in zones 6-9, it may go dormant in summer before blooming.

The familiar Florist's Cyclamen *(C. persica)* only grows outside in zones 9-10.

WHERE TO PLANT

Cyclamens need shade and summer dryness. This makes them ideal for planting below mature trees, where grass and many other plants do not thrive. Their abundant foliage and flowers will provide a much more satisfying view than a shaded, sparse lawn.

A shady bed along a foundation, where the soil is dry and alkaline, can be difficult to plant. The silver-marked leaves of Cyclamens will make an attractive groundcover, with the added bonus of pretty blooms.

Shady spots in a rock garden also make excellent settings for Cyclamens, as the good drainage will keep

The hardy Cyclamen coum wi

them thriving for years. Tuc them into protected crevice to maximize hardiness.

PERFECT PARTNERS

Choose companions, such as Ferns and fall-foliage shrubs, that like shady conditions and will not overwhelm the Cyclamens' delicate beauty.

Japanese Painted Fern shares the silvery cast on the leaves of many Cyclamens. Pair it with frilly-edged, dee pink 'Pearl Wave'.

Plant Trout Lilies and Dutchman's-breeches among fall-blooming, lavender-pink *C. mirabile* (zones 8-9). The wildflowers will die back as the Cyclamen emerges.

Carpet the ground unde a dwarf evergreen or small, red-leaved Japanese Maple

snowdrops in a woodland bed

with the tiny, pink flowers of miniature *C. alpinum.* It blooms in spring.

C. libanoticum blooms in early spring in zones 7-9. Its fragrant, rose-marked white blooms will offer a breathtaking end to winter when planted below a purple-flowering Redbud.

Nestled with Asparagus Ferns

PLANTING & AFTERCARE

YOU WILL NEED: ❏ Cyclamen tubers ❏ Spade ❏ Tarp ❏ Gravel ❏ Leaf mold ❏ Bone meal ❏ Lime

1 In early fall or mid-spring, prepare a planting area by digging out the soil to a depth of 8 in. and setting it aside on a large tarp.

2 Loosen soil in the bottom of bed. Improve drainage by spreading a 2 in. layer of gravel in bottom of planting area.

3 Refill hole with soil. Mix in 3 in. of leaf mold and one handful of bone meal per square foot. Add lime if soil is acidic.

4 Smooth the bed level with surrounding area. Set tubers, roots down, 4 in. apart, pressing lightly into soil. Water to settle soil.

5 Cover tubers with ½ in. of soil. Each spring, topdress Cyclamens with a sprinkling of bone meal and ½ in. of leaf mold.

Troubleshooter

Deep planting or heavy mulching can cause your Cyclamens to rot. Keep the planting clear of thick layers of fallen leaves.

Secrets of Success

BUYING HINTS

- **Buy plump, firm tubers** in early fall or spring, when they are dormant.
- **Avoid soft or mushy** Cyclamen tubers. Do not buy Cyclamen tubers with dry, stringy roots, as they will take longer to recover, establish, and bloom.

SUN & SOIL

- **Partial to full shade.** All Cyclamens do well in shade. *C. cilicium* will tolerate more sun than most types.
- **Well-drained, neutral** soil. Light, rich soil, such as that found in woodland areas, is ideal. Add lime to neutralize very acidic soils.

SPECIAL ADVICE

- **Cyclamens can take** several years to bloom well. As long as foliage emerges, blooms will follow.
- **Protect Cyclamens** from excess moisture, which can reduce blooms, by covering with a plastic sheet during periods of heavy rain.

 ## Seasonal Tips

 ## Plant Doctor

FALL
Planting & Maintaining
Plant tubers in early fall, as soon as they become available. Blooming plants may need watering in a dry season. Remove fallen leaves from the planting area.

LATE SUMMER
Thinning
Mature Cyclamens may self-seed freely. Without disturbing the established tubers, dig up seedlings and replant immediately in a freshly prepared bed *(below)*.

SPRING
Planting & Topdressing
Tubers of fall-blooming Cyclamens may be available in spring only; plant as soon as you get them. Topdress established plantings with bone meal and a thin layer of leaf mold or compost.

Cyclamen plants are occasionally bothered by Cyclamen mites. These minute pests eat into the plant's buds and tubers, distorting plant growth and preventing bloom. Control them with frequent dustings of fine sulfur purchased from a garden center.

Ivy-leaved Geraniums

Nonstop, bright blooms and glossy leaves

Season	Special Features	Best Conditions	
Annual	✓ Easy to grow	🌐 All zones	
✳ Flowers from spring through summer	✦ Fast growing	☀ Full sun to partial shade	Height: 6-30 in.
		🔧 Well-drained, slightly acidic soil	

◀ Spread: 2-3 ft. ⌐

Trails of Blooms

Choose either soothing or electric colors of Ivy-leaved Geraniums to illuminate summer scenes.

COLORS & VARIETIES

Ivy-leaved Geraniums are unparalleled for their bright flower clusters and glossy, succulent foliage. Their trailing stems and pointed, Ivy-like leaves provide cascades of color and 1-3 ft. mounds of greenery all summer long.

Single-blossomed plants, such as charming 'Rose Baby' and lilac 'Lila', burst into bloom in early spring in warm, protected areas and remain covered with dainty flowers until frost.

Ivy-leaved Geraniums with semi-double blooms, such as the fuchsia 'Beauty of Eastbourne', bear fewer blossoms, but they develop a winsome trailing habit. 'La France' is a striking mauve highlighted with white and purple veins.

Showier varieties of Ivy-leaved Geraniums include those with Rose-like, fully double flowers, such as rose

'Tavira' in a hanging basket

Deep pink 'Summer Showers'

pink 'Galilee', or variegated leaves, such as the pale rose 'Crocodile' with cream-veined leaves. Pale mauve 'L'Elégante' offers cream- or pink-edged leaves.

WHERE TO PLANT

The natural trailing habit of Ivy-leaved Geraniums is perfectly suited for use in hanging baskets, containers, and sloping beds.

On a balcony amid containers of dramatic foliage plants, set a classic urn filled to overflow with red-striped, white-flowered 'Rouletta' or the crimson-streaked blooms of 'Salmon Queen'.

Add splashes of poolside color by mixing different shades of red and pink in large containers. Use the red hues of 'Harvard' and 'Yale' in containers on wood decks.

In warm regions where they will overwinter, plant Ivy-leaved Geraniums on banks or hillsides in partial to

'Mini Cascade' Ivy-leaved Ger

full sun where they will provide abundant, year-roun color and greenery.

PERFECT PARTNERS

Ivy-leaved Geraniums mix well in hanging containers with other trailing plants. In beds, use them to accent th foliage of shrubs, Ferns, grasses, and taller perennial

For a showstopping scene and sensational color, spill mounds of the single-flowered 'Apricot Queen' over a stone retaining wall i front of the variegated leave and fragrant flowers of Japanese Pittosporum.

For a romantic look, mix compact 'Pink Gay Baby', delicate white Lobeli

...ums and Convolvulus sabatius

or Baby's Breath, and trailing, white-edged Ground Ivy in a hanging basket.

For stunning elegance, combine pink 'The Blush' with white Impatiens. Or dangle dark violet 'Comedy' over the edges of patio containers of Boxwood.

Geraniums coloring a wall

PLANTING & AFTERCARE

1 Scrub previously used 12 in. wide container with hot water and a mild bleach solution to eliminate plant residues and diseases.

2 Fill the container halfway with moistened, soilless potting mix that contains either peat moss or sterilized compost.

3 Moisten rootballs before removing from containers. Turn Ivy-leaved Geraniums upside down and push on bottoms to loosen.

4 Loosen roots; sever tightly twined ones. Set plants in container so tops are 1 in. below rim, 4 in. apart. Fill with soil and firm.

5 Water thoroughly. Allow soil to dry in between waterings. Fertilize and repeat recommended fertilizer doses regularly.

Tip

Ivy-leaved Geraniums will suffer in very hot sun. Provide some midday shade if temperatures rise above 85 degrees F.

Secrets of Success

BUYING HINTS

- **Buy healthy** nursery plants in bloom in spring. Select larger plants for gardens and smaller ones for hanging containers.
- **Avoid plants** that are leggy or have yellowed leaves, signs of root damage, or overwatering.

SUN & SOIL

- **Full to partial sun.** Ivy-leaved Geraniums flower well in full sun, but require some shade in containers.
- **Well-drained soil.** In beds, plant in average soil with added organic matter. Use commercial soil mixes in container plantings.

SPECIAL ADVICE

- **Do not place** plants close to walls, as they do not tolerate reflected heat well.
- **Ivy-leaved Geraniums** perform best when their roots are loosened at planting time, and plants are slightly crowded during the growing season.

 ## Seasonal Tips

LATE SPRING
Planning & Selecting
Wait for nursery offerings to bloom for the best color selection. Look for special varieties to blend with your garden scheme.

SUMMER
Maintaining & Watering
For a constant show of blooms, remove flower stems when most of a cluster has faded. If leaves yellow, water less often. If soil dries out completely, submerge container in a tub of water *(right)*.

FALL
Overwintering
Before the first frost, take tip cuttings from stems without flowers and root in moist vermiculite or sand. Overwinter Ivy-leaved Geraniums indoors in pots filled with moist sand.

Plant Doctor

Ivy-leaved Geraniums are usually pest-free, but may develop a stippled or flecked appearance from spider mite damage if stressed by drought. Overhead watering helps minor problems. Treat heavy infestations with an insecticidal soap spray.

Lantanas

Undulating drifts of constant color

Season	Special Features	Best Conditions	
Annual	Fast growing	Zones 9-10	
Flowers from spring to frost	Drought tolerant	Full sun	
	Attractive to wildlife	Well-drained, average soil	
	Poisonous		Height: 1-6 ft.
			Spread: 2-6 ft.

Trailing Blossoms

Lantanas' fast-growing, spreading stems bloom with abandon in sunny, bright colors.

COLORS & VARIETIES

Lantanas are loved for their easy care and continuous supply of rounded clusters of tiny, tubular blossoms that cover mounding plants. The pungent, deep green leaves are finely wrinkled and develop burgundy tones in cool weather. While Lantanas are grown as annuals in most regions, they become large, evergreen perennial shrubs in frost-free climates.

The vibrant blooms of the 3-6 ft. *Lantana camara* open gold, then turn orange or red; all colors often show at once. The somewhat hardier *L. montevidensis* bears lilac flowers on lower-growing, trailing stems.

Hybrid varieties bloom in a wide range of colors and often blend shades of yellow, red, and lavender. 'Radiation' is orange-red with touches of hot pink and yellow. The blooms of 'Festival' turn from a rich cream to deep pink.

Makes a colorful groundcover

WHERE TO PLANT

Seldom out of flower, fast-growing Lantanas are essential container plants for brightening patios and porches. As annuals (or, in warm areas as perennials), they are incomparable for their color and durability in mass plantings.

In a large planter box, add one Lantana to trail over the sides. Or, plant three together for a mounding and cascading sensation.

Along foundations or in annual beds, replace more common plants such as Petunias with Lantanas' multicolored blooms for color from spring to frost.

In tough situations such as salt-sprayed seaside banks, windy hillsides, and over dry retaining walls, Lantanas perform brilliantly. They grow vigorously in poor soils, flower freely in intense heat, and tolerate some drought as well as steamy humidity and rains.

In a bed with Alstroemerias,

PERFECT PARTNERS

The numerous colors and sizes of Lantana hybrids make it easy to dress up containers and add dimension to beds of annuals or perennials and mixed plantings.

Bright, bicolored L. camara

Lilac-pink L. montevidensis

PLANTING & AFTERCARE

YOU WILL NEED: ❏ Lantana plant ❏ 12 in. hanging container ❏ Drill ❏ Potting soil mix ❏ Water

1 **Select a container** at least 6 in. deep and 1 ft. in diameter that is durable, lightweight, and suitable for winter use inside.

2 **Add drainage holes** to bottom if none are present. Fill with 1-2 in. of moist potting soil. Water Lantana before repotting.

3 **Take plant out** of its nursery container and loosen circled roots. Set it in new pot with surface 1 in. below rim. Add soil and firm.

4 **Water well.** Allow soil to dry between future waterings. Pinch growing tips to encourage more blooms and prune to desired shape.

5 **Move Lantana** indoors to a bright windowsill when temperatures drop below 30 degrees F. Prune stems to promote blooms.

Tip

Water hanging plants daily during very hot or windy weather. If the soil dries out completely, submerge in pail of water.

e Anthemis, and Lavender

Complement large tubs of luxuriant, billowing Fountain Grass and majestic Miscanthus 'Yaku Jima' with the lavish yellow tones of compact 'Gold Rush'. Or, use the vivid yellow, pink, and purple flourishes offered by vigorous 'Confetti'.

In xeriscape (low-water) gardens, combine the gray-green foliage and tall, velvety spikes of Mexican Bush Sages with spreading mounds of 'White Lightning' Lantanas and gray Lavender Cottons.

Where plants must tolerate wind and salt spray in coastal gardens, use mounds of 'Lavender Swirl' and 'Lemon Swirl' Lantanas. Plant them with shrubby Lupines and dark purple 'Violetta' Statices.

Secrets of Success

BUYING HINTS

- **Buy plants** in bloom for best color selection. Choose upright plants for beds and trailing ones for containers.
- **Avoid Lantana plants** with woody stems. Do not buy any with leaf stippling or leaf spots, which indicate insect damage or disease.

SUN & SOIL

- **Full sun.** Sun-loving Lantanas must have bright light for abundant blooms. They easily withstand heat, humidity, and drought.
- **Well-drained, average** soil. Lantanas prefer sandy, well-drained soil on the dry side with low fertility.

SPECIAL ADVICE

- **In frost-free** climates, Lantanas are perennial and shrubby. In colder climates, they can be dug up, potted, pruned back severely, and moved inside for the winter.
- **Lantana flowers** attract butterflies, bees, and some beneficial predatory insects.

 ## Seasonal Tips

LATE WINTER
Sowing
Sow Lantana seeds in a cold frame or in six-packs indoors for spring blooms. Be patient; seeds often take 8-10 weeks to sprout.

SPRING
Maintaining
Transplant seedlings after last frost. When setting overwintered plants outside in spring, cut out older woody growth. Cut all stems back to 6-12 in. *(right).* If growth is slow, apply a half-strength balanced fertilizer.

SUMMER
Propagating
Enjoy new plants of your favorite varieties next spring by cutting 6 in. sections from tips of healthy stems without flowers. Root cuttings in moist sand or vermiculite and overwinter indoors.

 Plant Doctor

Mealybugs can be troublesome on Lantanas in warm areas. They form white, cottony masses and secrete honeydew that hosts a black fungus. Rinsing off foliage with water helps discourage them. Summer oils and insecticidal soaps are also effective.

Ornamental Kales

Giant, leafy rosettes in pastel hues

Season	Special Features	Best Conditions	
A Annual	✓ Easy to grow	🌐 All zones	
Colorful fall foliage	✦ Fast growing	☀ Full sun	Height: 8-18 in.
	X Edible leaves	Fertile, well-drained soil	◄ Spread: 12-15 in.

e an interesting autumn bed

The rosy pink centers and green outer leaves veined with pink of 'Osaka Pink' Ornamental Cabbages blend well with other cool-weather annuals, such as pink-flowered Stocks and white Sweet Alyssum.

Vibrant 'Red Feather'

PLANTING & AFTERCARE

YOU WILL NEED: ❏ Ornamental Kale seeds ❏ Soil ❏ Six-pack ❏ Compost ❏ Spading fork ❏ Mulch

1 Start seeds in early to mid-summer for fall display. Fill a clean six-pack with damp potting soil. Tap on hard surface to firm soil.

2 Place three seeds in each cell and cover with 1/4 in. of soil. Set container in a bright, sunny, warm spot at 60-65 degrees F.

3 Water when soil is dry. When seedlings have two sets of true leaves, thin to one plant per cell. Put in sun for three hours a day.

4 Before transplanting to the garden, work a 3 in. layer of compost and a sprinkling of fertilizer for vegetables into bed.

5 Set seedlings in garden when they are 3-4 in. tall, placing them 12 in. apart. Add a thin layer of mulch to conserve moisture.

Tip

Though bred mainly for looks rather than flavor, Ornamental Kale leaves are edible. Add small leaves to salads or use as a garnish.

Frilly Fall Foliage

The profuse foliage of Ornamental Kale seems to bloom with rich, deep colors.

COLORS & VARIETIES

The bright hues of Ornamental Kales do not come from blossoms but rather from the rosettes of frilly, white, pink, red, or magenta foliage framed by thick, blue-green outer leaves. The colors are strongest after the first frosts of fall, lasting until snowfall in cold climates and until spring in mild regions.

Feathery 'Red Peacock' Ornamental Kale grows to 18 in. with deeply serrated central leaves that range from glowing pink to dark red and green. 'White Peacock' is a more subtle selection with creamy white central leaves surrounded by large, green outer leaves.

Plants called Ornamental Cabbage are quite similar, but generally have smoother leaf edges and form tighter heads than Ornamental Kale. They are grown and used in the same way. 'Tokyo

Brilliant 'Pipeon Red'

Hybrid' Ornamental Cabbage features central splashes of red, pink, or white on sturdy, 12 in. plants.

WHERE TO PLANT

The bold forms and colors of Ornamental Kales add a cheery and decorative touch to beds, borders, containers, and fall vegetable gardens.

In early fall, replace a flower bed of fading summer annuals with groups of the lacy-leaved, 8 in. tall 'Nagoya Red' and 'Nagoya White' Ornamental Kales.

'Frizzy', another compact variety, grows 8 in. tall with a 12 in. spread. Its ruffled pink or white leaves make a charming edging for an autumn garden of salad greens, Beets, and vegetable (garden-variety) Kales.

For a light-hearted greeting near an entry, plant 'White Sparrow' Ornamental Kales singly in 8 in. pots. Or, group several plants in a larger container.

A formal Kale garden

Assorted Kales and Pansies

PERFECT PARTNERS

The richly colored foliage of Ornamental Kales provides an interesting and unusual contrast to many plants that flower in autumn.

Plant the aptly named 'White Kamome' Ornamental Kale to diversify the form and complement a bed of lavender-blue 'Professor Kippenburg' New York Asters or bronze- and gold-hued Chrysanthemums.

The leaves of 'Red Chidori' Ornamental Kales are a complex blend of rosy pink centers with darker magenta edges. They make a stunning combination with the tall, coppery rose spikes of Fountain Grass.

Secrets of Success

BUYING HINTS

- **Buy Ornamental Kale** plants in 4 in. or gallon containers in early fall. After the first frost, the foliage will show its bright colors.
- **Avoid plants** starting to form flower stalks, as the foliage effect is ruined once Ornamental Kale blooms.

SUN & SOIL

- **Full sun.** Ornamental Kale grows best in full sun, but the plants will tolerate a few hours of shade.
- **Fertile,** well-drained soil. Add organic matter, such as compost or well-rotted manure, plus a sprinkling of fertilizer before planting.

SPECIAL ADVICE

- **Make the most of** Ornamental Kale's vivid colors by planting it in front of a solid green hedge.
- **Ornamental Kale** can be grown for the early spring garden, but it often forms a flower stalk as soon as warm weather arrives.

 Seasonal Tips

 Plant Doctor

SPRING

Ordering seeds

For special Ornamental Kale varieties, order seeds from mail-order catalogs.

EARLY SUMMER

Direct sowing

Instead of starting seeds in containers, you can sow directly in the garden where they are to grow, in soil prepared with compost.

EARLY FALL

Planting & Fertilizing

Set out nursery-bought plants in early fall. Feed new and established Ornamental Kale plants monthly with a fertilizer for vegetables, following the directions on the label. If rain is lacking, water plants regularly (*below*).

Cabbageworms, small, light green caterpillars that are the larval form of the Cabbage butterfly, can quickly destroy your young Cabbage plants. Use a spray containing Bt, which is toxic to caterpillars but safe for other creatures.

Pansies

Blossoms with charming faces and velvety texture

Season	Special Features	Best Conditions	
A Annual	✕ Edible flowers	⊕ All zones	
❋ Flowers in winter, spring, or summer	✂ Good for cutting	☀ Full sun to partial shade	 Height: 6-8 in.
	✓ Easy to grow	🔬 Well-drained soil	← Spread: 6-8 in. ↵

Flowers with Personality

A welcome sight in any season, Pansies offer a rainbow of bright colors and bicolors.

COLORS & VARIETIES

Pansies are invaluable for color in the garden during the cooler parts of the year. The flat, 1-4 in. blooms, available in every color of the rainbow, are often marked with contrasting, face-like centers. Pansies open mid-spring into summer in the North and fall through spring in the South and Southwest on slender stems above narrow leaves.

The '**Majestic Giants**' strain has extra-large flowers, up to 4 in. across, with the classic Pansy face. Available in combinations of purple, yellow, white, red, or blue, these Pansies grow on compact, 7 in. plants and are tolerant of heat and cold.

The '**Crown Series**' has "faceless", solid-colored blossoms. The 2-3 in. wide flowers appear early in the season in many shades, including orange, scarlet, blue, purple, and yellow.

For unusual, dramatic colors of Pansies, look for glowing orange 'Padparadja' or 'Black Devil', which features jet black blossoms.

WHERE TO PLANT

With low mounds of tidy foliage and bountiful blooms, Pansies work well in beds and borders, as edging plants, and in containers.

Plant a wide swathe of the 'Deep Blue' selection of 'Crystal Bowl' Pansies to flow through a border of flowers or groups of low shrubs.

A combination of solid orange and white-and-yellow Pansies from the 'Universal Series' makes a trim edge for a bed of tall Bearded Irises.

Fill a strawberry pot with the ruffled, tawny hues of 'Imperial Antique Shades' Pansies for an elegant accent on a patio or terrace.

PERFECT PARTNERS

Since Pansies bloom in such a wide range of colors, it is easy to devise many beautiful

Pansies and Rhododendrons

combinations for the cool-season garden.

'**Watercolor**' Pansies offer a mix of soft blue, pink, salmon, apricot, yellow, and white shades that blend well with pastel-flowering plants. Paint a soft-hued bed by mixing 'Watercolors' with pale yellow 'Wedding Bell' Snapdragons, Dianthus 'Pink Jewel', and Creeping Phlox 'White Delight'.

For a sky blue planting in early spring, pair 'Maxim Marina' Pansy, which has dark blue-faced blossoms edged in white, with pale blue Forget-me-nots.

Pansies create a neat and lovely carpet underneath taller flowers. Use the 3 in. wide, pink-and-white flowers

The bicolored 'Joker'

The striking 'Black Devil'

pretty picture in pink

Lovely with Chrysanthemums

of 'Imperial Pink' below deep-hued blooms, such as the 2 ft., intense blue Delphinium 'Blue Mirror' or 1 ft., deep purple Veronica 'Kapitan'. The Pansy's full, open blooms offer a delightful pale contrast.

PLANTING & AFTERCARE

YOU WILL NEED: ❑ Pansy seeds ❑ Six-packs ❑ Potting soil ❑ Newspaper ❑ Fertilizer ❑ Mulch

1 Plant Pansy seeds eight to ten weeks ahead of your desired time for transplanting them outdoors. Sow seeds in clean six-packs.

2 Sow two or three seeds per cell. Cover with 1/8 in. of moist potting soil. Cover six-packs with damp, folded newspaper.

3 Place six-packs in a cool, shaded spot. Water when the soil feels dry. Remove newspaper when the seeds sprout.

4 Thin seedlings to one per cell when they are 1 in. tall. Water as needed and feed with diluted liquid fertilizer each week.

5 Transplant Pansies outdoors in late fall in zones 7-11, or in early spring in zones 3-6. Space plants 6-8 in. apart.

Tip

In the first warm days of spring, cut Pansies back to stimulate new growth and blooms. Clear away any winter mulch.

Secrets of Success

BUYING HINTS

- **Buy Pansy plants** in early spring or fall in six-packs, or purchase seeds. Choose stocky plants with dark green foliage and many buds, but few or no blooms.
- **Avoid Pansies with** yellowed foliage, many flowers, or any seedpods.

SUN & SOIL

- **Full sun to partial** shade. In cool climates, Pansies do well in full sun. In hot areas, they flower longer if provided with some afternoon shade.
- **Well-drained soil.** Add organic matter to improve drainage and enrich the soil.

SPECIAL ADVICE

- **Pansy blooms** are edible. Use them as a garnish or add the petals to salads.
- **Seeds of non-hybrid** varieties are easy to harvest. Let plants form seedpods. Pick when dry. Store in paper bags in a dry spot until planting time.

 ## Seasonal Tips

 ## Plant Doctor

EARLY SPRING
Planting & Maintaining
Plant new Pansies. Feed all plants with a slow-release fertilizer. Pull up weeds when they are small to avoid overwhelming young Pansies. Add mulch to block out weeds and retain moisture.

SPRING—SUMMER
Pinching back
To prolong blooming season, pick faded flowers before they set seed *(right)*. If the Pansy plant is allowed to use its energy making seeds, it will produce fewer flowers.

Pinch back leggy stems and 1-2 in. of foliage every few weeks to keep plants neat.

FALL
Planting
In mild climates, set out new plants through the fall.

Pansies may suffer from stem and root rot, which is indicated by leaves that turn yellow and die, and soft roots that eventually rot. Prevent by planting in well-drained soil. Discard dead or dying Pansy plants.

Perennial Primroses

A vibrant, early-spring bloomer for low-light areas

Season	Special Features	Best Conditions	
P Perennial	✛ Naturalizes well	🌐 Zones 4-9	
✹ Flowers from early to late spring	✓ Easy care	☀ Filtered shade	↕ Height: 6-12 in.
		🖐 Moist, slightly acidic soil	◄— Spread: 4-18 in.

Shade-loving Color

Transform dark, damp garden nooks into bright spots with the luminous shades of Primroses.

COLORS & VARIETIES

Perennial Primroses bloom in a wide range of purples, yellows, reds, pinks, and whites. These low-growing plants boast rosettes of foliage that send up blooms in early and mid-spring. *Primula veris* grows nodding, 6-9 in. wide, bright yellow blooms. The foliage dies back in the summer.

English Primroses (*P. vulgaris*) offer smaller, 1 ½ in. wide flowers. These radiant blooms are available in a wide range of colors.

Japanese Primroses (*P. japonica*) are among the easiest to grow. They feature slightly wrinkled, light green leaves and flowers in brilliant shades of red and white.

WHERE TO PLANT

These shade-loving flowers do best when planted in moist, shadowy areas with rich, slightly acidic soil. Plant them in filtered light close to other acid-loving plants.

'Red Shades' Primroses

On a patio, decorate with several terra-cotta pots full of vibrant Primroses for the first color of the season.

The north side of a house is often one of the shadiest and dampest areas in the garden. Plant a row of 'Crescendo Hybrids' along the base of a white stucco wall for a vibrant attraction.

Under the spreading canopy of a tree, or beneath the foliage of other shade-lovers, Primroses provide lively splashes of color.

PERFECT PARTNERS

Primroses marry well with other brightly colored flowers and are dashing with shade-loving foliage plants.

Plant a colorful, shady perennial flower bed with the purple, yellow-eyed 'Wanda', deep blue Forget-me-nots, fiery red Bleeding Hearts, and coral-pink Astilbes. This design offers brilliant rainbow shades.

The rainbow hues of English

Let Primroses peek out from underneath blooming shrubs that grow in the sam‹ acidic soil that Primroses prefer. Plant the deep red 'Miller's Crimson' under a border of Rhododendrons, Azaleas, and Camellias.

Brighten dark corners b‹ planting groups of Primrose‹ among Ferns, Hostas, and other foliage plants that can tolerate moist, low-light areas. Allow the white, pink‹ or red hues of the 'Juliana Hybrids' to fuse with a rang‹ of greens in varying texture‹

Use early-blooming English Primroses as color

The gold 'Sunshine Suzy'

mroses

underneath the tall stems of Tulips. Fuse the magenta hues of 'Barnhaven Doubles' with 'White Emperor' Tulips for an exciting design.

'Juno Blue Light' with Daffodils

PLANTING & AFTERCARE

YOU WILL NEED: ❏ Perennial Primrose plants ❏ Garden hoe ❏ Compost ❏ Wood chips

1 Dig a trench for the Primroses that is 6 in. deep and 8 in. long. As you dig, loosen the soil along the sides of the trench.

2 Add two cups of well-rotted compost and mix with the soil. Add a cup of water to ensure the mix is moistened well.

3 Remove the plant from its pot by turning it upside down and knocking its rim on a hard surface. Loosen rootball with fingers.

4 Set plant in hole so that it sits at the same level as it did in its container. Place in the middle of the trench. Fill with soil and firm.

5 Water well and cover with a 1 in. layer of wood chips. Water regularly during dry weather, so that the soil is continually moist.

Tip

Cover Primroses with fir branches in fall and mulch heavily in cold winter areas to protect from severe weather.

Secrets of Success

BUYING HINTS

- **Buy Primrose plants** in bloom in spring so that you can verify their flower color. Look for plants that are robust and green.
- **Avoid Primroses** with ragged leaves. Do not buy plants with brown or black lesions on the foliage.

SUN & SOIL

- **Partial shade.** Perennial Primroses prefer filtered sun, but in mild climates with plenty of water, they can survive in full sun.
- **Rich, moist, slightly** acidic soil. Primroses grow the brightest blooms in soil rich with organic matter.

SPECIAL ADVICE

- **If growing seedlings** indoors, make sure pots are kept at 70 degrees F. or seeds may not sprout.
- **Use potted Primroses** in a windowbox. Remove pots in summer after they stop blooming and transplant into the garden.

 Seasonal Tips

 Plant Doctor

FALL
Watering & Protecting
Water Perennial Primroses deeply if autumn rains are scarce. Cover the plants with a 1 in. layer of organic mulch and fir boughs in cold winter areas to protect from severe wind and weather.

SPRING
Buying & Baiting
Purchase Primroses in bloom so you can verify their color and plant them out into the garden or in containers on the patio or deck. During periods of wet weather, purchase snail and slug bait to place around Perennial Primroses and prevent any damage *(below)*.

SUMMER
Watering
Keep well watered in heat.

The fungal infection leaf spot can affect Primroses in the cool, moist climates that they prefer. Look for dark brown lesions on yellowing leaves. Remove and destroy any infected foliage. Dig up and divide Primroses to aid in air circulation.

Poeticus Daffodils

Pure, fragrant blooms are the essence of poetry

Season	Special Features	Best Conditions	
Flowers in mid- to late spring	Easy to grow Good for cutting Fragrant	Zones 3-10 Full sun to partial shade Well-drained to moist soil	 Height: 12-18 in. Spread: 6-8 in.

Sweetly Simple Charmers

The elegant spring blooms combine the grace of wildflowers with a haunting perfume.

COLORS & VARIETIES

There are few varieties in the Poeticus division of Daffodils, but all are choice plants. These Daffodils are fragrant and feature crisp, white petals centered with small, yellow, red-edged cups.

The original Poet's Daffodil is 'Pheasant's Eye', with a spot of bright green in the center of its tiny cup. It offers the strongest fragrance of all, with a hint of spice underscoring the sweetness.

The old variety 'Actaea' is the largest of the Poeticus varieties with 4 in. wide blooms on 18 in stems. Its size, and the way it perfumes the air, makes it ideal for formal flower beds.

While there are no true miniatures in the group, perky 'Cantabile' comes close. Only 12 in. tall, it is perfect for adding fragrance to a windowbox.

Perfect with Forsythia

WHERE TO PLANT

Grow these beauties close to the house to enjoy their wonderful fragrance. Poet's Daffodils bloom fairly late in good weather, so be sure to time them to coincide with other late-blooming plants.

Take advantage of the shade tolerance of Poeticus Daffodils. Enjoy the fragrance of these pale beauties as you stroll in the warm spring air by lining a woodland path or edging a partially shaded bed or border.

Naturalize them in a corner where the grass can be left through summer. Try this even in moist spots, as this group does not need the sharp drainage that most spring bulbs demand.

In outdoor containers or beds near the door, you will enjoy the perfume as you come and go. Protected spots and raised beds will both emphasize the fragrance.

Delicate 'Pheasant's Eye'

Poeticus Daffodils are charm

PERFECT PARTNERS

The simple beauty of Poeticus Daffodils never overwhelms, yet it never goes unnoticed even in the most tumultuous floral display. While they work in any setting, it is especially nice to add these bulbs to plantings that lack fragrance

The clean, white petals of 'Milan' will make peace between the riotous colors of Single Late Tulips, such as 'Golden Harvest' and sultry red 'Balalaika', while supplying a sweet perfume.

In a shady setting, plant groups of fragrant 'Felindre' among clumps of white-edged 'Northern Halo' Hostas. They unfurl just as the Daffodils finish blooming

naturalized in a meadow

With the lovely but unscented 'Swan Lake' white Spirea, Poeticus Daffodils will add an extra dimension. 'Actea' is the variety that offers the size and substance to suit such a shrub.

The stately blooms of 'Actaea'

PLANTING & AFTERCARE

YOU WILL NEED: ❏ Poeticus Daffodil bulbs ❏ Bulb planter ❏ Twigs ❏ Bulb fertilizer ❏ Mulch

1 Plant Daffodils in early fall. Along a woodland path, push in twigs to mark placement of bulbs in thick, irregular clusters.

2 View placement of twigs from all angles to ensure it looks natural. The bulbs should look as if they have colonized the area.

3 Use a bulb planter to remove a plug of soil at each marker. Sprinkle a pinch of bulb fertilizer in hole and insert bulb, pointed end up.

4 Replace the soil in the hole and firm it. When all bulbs are planted, water well and top with an inch of compost or other mulch.

Tip

5 Remove faded flowers but leave foliage to die back naturally. Topdress with a sprinkling of fertilizer and an inch of compost every fall.

If you expect good rainfall within the week, skip watering newly planted bulbs. Be sure to water if it fails to rain.

Secrets of Success

BUYING HINTS

- **Buy the largest bulbs** available. Large bulbs that look like two joined together will usually send up two blooming stalks.
- **Avoid soft** or moldy Poeticus Daffodil bulbs, as these are signs of decay. Do not buy any bruised bulbs.

SUN & SOIL

- **Full sun** to partial shade. Poeticus varieties tolerate more shade than other Daffodils but need at least three hours of sun each day.
- **Well-drained** to moist soil. Avoid planting in soggy areas, but these bulbs prefer soil that is evenly moist.

SPECIAL ADVICE

- **Plant Poeticus Daffodils** in a large tub. Keep it in an unheated, protected place until spring. It will bloom weeks before bulbs in beds.
- **For the most natural** look, avoid "naturalizing mixtures" and plant a single variety of Poeticus Daffodils.

 ## Seasonal Tips

EARLY FALL
Planting & Fertilizing
Plant new Poeticus Daffodil bulbs. Fertilize established plantings with a sprinkling of bulb fertilizer, scratching it into the surface soil. Mulch bulbs with a layer of compost or leaf mold.

WINTER
Planting
In zones 9-10, plant bulbs outdoors after chilling them in the refrigerator for eight weeks. Or, purchase pre-chilled bulbs that are ready to be planted.

SPRING
Deadheading & Dividing
Remove faded flowers but not leaves. Wait until leaves yellow before removing. Divide crowded bulbs after the foliage has yellowed but before it disappears *(below)*.

 ## Plant Doctor

If the flowers of your Poeticus Daffodils shrivel and turn brown before they open, they may be infested with thrips. These pests are so tiny they can only be seen under a magnifying glass. Remove any infested plant parts and spray with insecticidal soap to control.

'Rainbow's End'

A Miniature Rose with elegant blooms

Season	Special Features	Best Conditions	
✳ Flowers all summer	🕷 Disease resistant ✂ Good for cutting	🌐 Zones 4-10 ☀ Full sun 🔨 Well-drained, humus-rich soil	 ◀ Spread: 8-24 in. Height: 10-14 in. ▲

Sun-colored Blooms

Golden blooms and a full form make 'Rainbow's End' ideal for a container or garden bed.

COLORS & FORM

The hallmark of 'Rainbow's End' is its dazzling flowers. The flowers rarely grow more than 1 ½ in., but they feature the elegant, high-centered form found on champion Hybrid Tea Roses.

The golden yellow petals are edged with light pink accents that deepen to a rich fuchsia under prolonged exposure to direct sunlight. The blooms on a 'Rainbow's End' will remain entirely yellow if they are grown in shade or under artificial light indoors.

The beautiful blooms of these Miniature Roses are framed by glossy, emerald green foliage. 'Rainbow's End' grows in a compact, bushy form with well-balanced proportions and an attractive shape. The flowers seem to unfold from the bush.

'Rainbow's End' in a bed

Blooms in various stages

'Rainbow's End' in a containe

The Rose and blue Lobelia

WHERE TO PLANT

'Rainbow's End' exudes warmth wherever you place it in the garden. Like other Miniature Roses, its small size makes it ideal for a container.

In a sunny border, plant 'Rainbow's End' as a low edging. Plant a triangle of 'Rainbow's End' plants next to a similar planting of 'Over the Rainbow' Roses, which have the reverse coloration.

Accent a small decorative pot with this compact beauty. 'Rainbow's End' will grow about 14-18 in. tall, and can

be grown as easily indoors as it can on a patio. Set the container by a sunny window when the weather cools to prolong the blooming season

As a tall groundcover, 'Rainbow's End' can fill out a slope with bushy growth and riveting color. Prune plants low to help them spread.

PERFECT PARTNERS

The 'Rainbow's End' Rose is a good match for most single color flowers.

Contrast the golden hue of 'Rainbow's End' with the

PLANTING & AFTERCARE

1 **Line the bottom** of the pot with a 2-3 in. layer of gravel. Add a layer of potting mix to the bottom of the pot and form it into a cone.

2 **Snip off** any twisted, broken, or dead roots with a pair of scissors. Cut back long roots, so that they are all about the same length.

3 **Spread the Rose's** roots over the cone of soil. Slowly fill the container with soil, firming to eliminate air pockets as you go.

4 **Make sure the area** where the canes join the main stem sits 2 in. higher than soil level. Water well and mulch with peat moss.

5 **After 'Rainbow's End'** stops blooming, cut its branches back to the lowest, unopened flower bud for vigorous, renewed growth the following year.

Tip

If you prefer slightly larger blooms, pinch off buds when they emerge until there is only one bud per branch.

...arden with Tuberous Begonias

bright blue of trailing Lobelia. The Lobelia's lush, spreading growth is ideal for softening the lines of a windowbox or other container planted with a single 'Rainbow's End'.

Tuberous Begonias look like Roses. Plant the yellow, red-edged blooms of 'Santa Paula' with 'Rainbow's End'.

Other Roses can make excellent partners for 'Rainbow's End'. Plant the Rose at the base of similarly colored Hybrid Teas. Try surrounding a single Hybrid Tea 'Peace' Rose with several 'Rainbow's End' Roses.

Secrets of Success

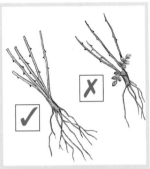

BUYING HINTS

- **Buy bareroot** Roses in spring. Look for plants with at least three canes. Buy container-grown plants in spring or summer.
- **Avoid 'Rainbow's End'** Roses that have dead or dry-looking canes, and those with new growth.

SUN & SOIL

- **Full sun.** 'Rainbow's End' flourishes under at least six hours of direct sun per day.
- **Rich, well-drained soil.** 'Rainbow's End' relies heavily on its soil, so it pays to add a generous amount of organic material, such as compost, before planting.

SPECIAL ADVICE

- **Use a dark, rich-colored** mulch around 'Rainbow's End' to show off its pastel blooms. Mulch with cocoa hull, which has both the smell and color of chocolate.
- **Put individual blooms** in tiny vases as unique place settings for the dinner table.

Seasonal Tips

FIRST SPRING
Planting
Plant bareroot Roses as soon as you buy them in spring. Plant container-grown Roses in spring or summer, but never plant them during extremely hot weather.

SUMMER
Fertilizing
Fertilize every six weeks with a well-balanced Rose food until late summer. Sprinkle compost or well-rotted manure alongside your 'Rainbow's End' weekly.

FALL
Protecting
As the weather cools, remove any yard debris from around your 'Rainbow's End'. Provide protection in cold climates. Mound mulch around the base of the Rose and cover with a burlap sack.

NEXT SPRING
Pruning
Prune your 'Rainbow's End' sparingly. Remove dead wood, but do not cut back more than half the length of a healthy Rose cane.

Plant Doctor

Japanese beetles are brown insects about the size of a nickel. They chew holes through the Rose's leaves and flowers. Pick them off 'Rainbow's End', or shake them out of the blooms into a jar of rubbing alcohol. You can also find Japanese beetle traps at most nurseries.

Scented Geraniums
Star-shaped blooms framed by aromatic leaves

Season	*Special Features*	*Best Conditions*	
A Annual	✓ Easy care	🌐 All zones	 Height: 12-36 in. Spread: 12-24 in.
✳ Flowers all summer until first frost	🕷 Disease and insect resistant	✳ Full sun	
	✗ Some varieties: edible leaves	🔨 Well-drained soil	

Fragrant Foliage into Fall

Perfumed leaves and dainty blooms make these Geraniums ideal for containers or beds.

COLORS & VARIETIES

Scented Geranium plants are actually species of the family *Pelargonium*. They feature small, star-shaped blooms in shades of pink, purple, or white. Their fragrant foliage needs only to be brushed to give off the scents ranging from chocolate and Rose, to Pine and citrus fruits.

The 'Rose-scented' Geranium (*P. graveolens*) bears soft, ruffled leaves that release a spicy, Rose aroma. This variety's leaves, like the

The red-flecked 'Freckles'

Scented Geraniums in border

leaves of many Scented Geraniums, are edible.

Scented Geraniums also come in variegated forms. *P. crispum* 'Variegatum' is a Lemon-scented variety with small lilac flowers. It has green leaves edged with cream-colored streaks.

WHERE TO PLANT

Scented Geraniums add a distinctive element to any garden site, although they are usually placed in containers. You can plant a group in a bed of perennials or allow their scent to float into the kitchen from a windowbox.

Grouped in beds, the bushy, compact form of 'Royal Oak' is graceful with dark green leaves accented in brown. Its mauve blooms, unique foliage, and spicy fragrance are an enchanting addition to any garden bed.

Create a special terra-cotta container garden with Rose-scented *P. capitatum,* featuring pink flowers, and 'Old Spice' for a spicy musk fragrance and compact form with crinkle-edged leaves. Line up the pots in a row on a brick wall, or position them to border the edge of a patio where their delicious scents can be fully enjoyed.

In hanging baskets, use 'Snowy Nutmeg' with its broad, sweetly spice-scented leaves. Hang your basket near a doorway so that anyone who passes by will be treated to the delicious bouquet.

Scented Geraniums planted be

PERFECT PARTNERS

The bushy growth habit and attractive foliage of Scented Geraniums make them good companions for a host of other flowering plants.

Enjoy the colors and scent of candycanes in your windowbox by planting white Alyssum and red Petunias with Peppermint-scented *P. tomentosum*. The rich green leaves and small, white blooms of this Scented Geranium will provide a lush backdrop to the contrasting red-and-white color scheme.

For a graceful pastel color combination, plant the pale purple 'Mabel Grey' with lavender Petunias and violet Impatiens. The subtle Lemon

d the silver foliage of Senecio

fragrance of 'Mabel Grey' will enhance the cool colors of this planting, while its rough, serrated leaves provide exciting textures.

Orange Geranium blooms

PLANTING & AFTERCARE

YOU WILL NEED: ❑ Scented Geranium ❑ Scissors ❑ Clear glass container ❑ Potting soil ❑ Trowel ❑ Pot

1 In early fall, cut off a healthy, 4 in. long shoot from a Geranium. Remove lower leaves, and place in a glass container full of water.

2 Grow the new plant indoors over winter in a sunny window. Plant in a pot once cutting grows a full set of healthy roots.

3 Plant your Geranium outdoors in late spring to early summer, digging a hole in your garden large enough to accommodate the roots.

4 Set plant in hole so that the plant sits at the same level as it was before. Replace soil and firm gently without touching the stem.

5 Water at soil level sparingly to avoid stem rot. Remove blooms as they wilt. Fertilize once a month during growing season.

Troubleshooter

If potted Geranium root cuttings begin to turn black, use less water to keep soil barely moist.

Secrets of Success

BUYING HINTS

- **Buy bushy plants** with many buds in 4 in. pots. Choose ones with healthy-looking, lush, green foliage.
- **Avoid plants** that are tall and leggy with yellowing leaves. Scented Geranium stems with black bases may indicate root rot.

SUN & SOIL

- **Full sun.** A half-day of sun is enough for Geraniums to produce blooms, but they prefer full-sun exposure.
- **Well-drained soil.** They do not need very fertile soil, but Geraniums will suffer if soil is soggy. Improve poor drainage before planting.

SPECIAL ADVICE

- **For a sweet potpourri,** mix dried and crushed Scented Geranium leaves with Lavender, Rosemary, Orris root, and scented oil.
- **Crowd Geraniums** into pots that are a bit too small for the plants, and they will produce more blooms.

 Seasonal Tips

 Plant Doctor

SPRING
Planting
Prepare Geranium beds by improving drainage. Add sand or compost to clay soils. Plant seedlings in garden once all danger of frost has passed.

SUMMER
Planting & Deadheading
In early summer, plant your Geraniums outside in larger pots or beds *(right)*. Regularly remove the plants' faded flowers and foliage. Fertilize Geraniums that are growing in containers, using an all-purpose fertilizer every two weeks.

FALL
Propagating
Before the first frost, take cuttings from plants growing in your garden to grow inside over the winter.

Geraniums can develop a disease called root rot. Signs include plants that wilt even though their soil feels damp. Dig up and discard infected plants and improve drainage by growing in raised beds, adding compost to soil, or growing in pots.

Schizanthus

Colorful clouds of fluttering flowers

Season	*Special Features*	*Best Conditions*	
A Annual	✓ Easy to grow	🌐 All zones	
❋ Flowers in summer and early fall	✂ Good for cutting	☀ Full sun to partial shade	Height: 8-18 in.
		🔱 Fertile, well-drained soil	◄ Spread: 10-12 in.

Fanciful Blooms

Plant Schizanthus for masses of Orchid-like summer flowers plus delicate, lacy foliage.

COLORS & VARIETIES

The popular names "Butterfly Flower" and "Poor Man's Orchid" help describe the tropical-looking, lobed flowers of Schizanthus. They have wonderful multicolored markings on pink, rose, salmon, carmine, lavender, or white backgrounds. Light green, feathery foliage complements the colorful blossoms perfectly.

Schizanthus 'Angel Wings' forms neat, pyramid-shaped plants, 14 in. tall, blooming in shades of pink, cream, violet, or rose with a contrasting yellow center.

Flowering in deep hues spanning the entire color range, the striped petals of 15 in. 'Sweet Lips' lighten near the edges, intensifying the veined centers.

WHERE TO PLANT

Schizanthus is excellent for beds and borders in areas

Containers along a stairway

where summers are relatively cool. It also makes a colorful accent in windowboxes, hanging baskets, half-barrels, and other containers.

Try massing Schizanthus along steps or at the edge of a terrace or patio, where the interesting and colorful blossoms can be enjoyed at close range.

Plant dwarf Schizanthus 'Star Parade', which reaches a mere 8 in. tall, as a charming and unusual edging for a mixed bed of annuals and perennials.

In addition to container plantings for beautiful outdoor summer blooms, Schizanthus also grows well indoors in cool rooms for late-winter flowers.

PERFECT PARTNERS

The complementary colors of Schizanthus flowers enhance virtually any summertime combination of bright-

Mixed varieties of Schizanthu

flowering shrubs, annuals, and perennials.

For a mix of colorful annuals that all grow best in cool summer climates, plant 12-15 in. 'Dwarf Bouquet Mixed' Schizanthus with cornflower blue Swan River Daisies, hot pink Clarkias, rich blue Annual Larkspurs, and 'Orange Prince' Violas.

For a simple but very effective trio, set off the rich colors of 'Hit Parade' Schizanthus, an extra bushy strain that grows to 1 ft., with an edging of soft, silvery gray Lamb's-ears and white, airy Baby's Breath.

Fill a hanging basket to overflowing with radiant pinks, white, blues, and greens by combining 'Disco'

Bicolored 'Hit Parade'

PLANTING & AFTERCARE

YOU WILL NEED: ❑ Schizanthus seedlings in trays ❑ Spading fork ❑ Rake ❑ Compost ❑ Fertilizer ❑ Mulch

1 **For a mass planting** or edging of Schizanthus, prepare planting bed after last frost. Use a spading fork to loosen soil to 8 in. deep.

2 **Spread 2-3 in.** of compost over area plus all-purpose fertilizer applied according to label directions. Fork amendments into soil.

3 **Rake soil smooth.** Dig holes a little wider than rootball for each plant. Space holes 5 in. apart for dwarf varieties, 8 in. for others.

4 **Place the seedlings** in the holes, setting them at the same depth they grew in the trays. Firm soil gently around the plants.

5 **Water well** with gentle spray, making sure to moisten entire rootball and surrounding soil. Spread mulch around the plants.

Tip

Taller Schizanthus varieties will produce more flowers if you pinch back the growing tips when plants are 8 in. tall.

with Forget-me-nots

Schizanthus, a variety bred especially for pots, with a white-flowered Zonal Geranium, trailing 'Lilac Fountains' Lobelias, and variegated English Ivies.

Violet form of 'Angel Wings'

Secrets of Success

BUYING HINTS

- **Buy seedlings** in six-packs or 4 in. pots. Look for young, bushy plants that are not yet in flower.
- **Avoid buying** overgrown Schizanthus plants with spindly or drooping stems. Do not buy plants with yellowed foliage.

SUN & SOIL

- **Full sun to partial** shade. Schizanthus plants do not grow or bloom well in intense heat.
- **Fertile, well-drained** soil. Amend the soil with fertilizer and compost to add nutrients and ensure adequate drainage.

SPECIAL ADVICE

- **To ensure the longest** display of blooms, set out new Schizanthus plants every few weeks from late spring until mid-summer.
- **Schizanthus seeds** started in the fall and grown under lights indoors over winter will flower by spring.

 ## *Seasonal Tips*

LATE WINTER
Starting seeds indoors
Sow seeds 8-12 weeks before last frost in damp potting mix in flats or six-packs. Barely cover the seeds with potting mix. As darkness aids germination, cover container with cardboard until seeds sprout, in 7-14 days *(right)*. Plant out after last frost.

EARLY SUMMER
Watering & Fertilizing
Water when the top inch of soil is dry. Fertilize monthly with an all-purpose liquid fertilizer, diluted according to label directions.

MID-SUMMER
Staking
In windy areas, it is usually necessary to stake taller varieties of Schizanthus to prevent breaking of stems heavy with buds.

 ## *Plant Doctor*

Schizanthus may suffer from aster yellows disease, which is transmitted by leafhoppers. Symptoms are yellowed foliage and distorted flowers. Remove and destroy any infected plants. Apply rotenone to kill leafhoppers when you see them on Schizanthus.

Sweet Peas

Fragrant, old-fashioned favorites

Season	*Special Features*	*Best Conditions*	
A Annual	Fast growing	All zones	
Flowers in summer or early fall	Fragrant	Full sun	Height: 1-8 ft.
	Good for cutting	Well-drained, rich soil	
	Good for trellis		Spread: 1-2 ft.

Lavish Bouquet Factories

With regular watering and feeding, Sweet Peas amply reward your efforts.

COLORS & VARIETIES

Enchanting fragrance, silky petals, and clear colors are the joyful trademarks of annual Sweet Peas *(Lathyrus odoratus)*. They are available in a wide variety of colors, including shades of red, pink, white, lavender, salmon, blue, and bicolors. The traditional types climb to 6 ft. or more; newer hybrids include low-growing, bushy types as well as more heat-resistant varieties.

Colorful bed with Sweet Peas

Sweet Peas thrive in cool weather. In cold climates, they can be summer annuals; where winters are mild, grow them for early spring color. In hot-summer areas, choose heat-resistant varieties, such as 'Galaxy', and plant them as early as possible.

Early-flowering types mature more quickly than other Sweet Peas. 'Early Multiflora' and 'Early Mammoth' are examples of early-flowering Sweet Peas. Both offer an assortment of red, pink, white, blue, and purple blossoms.

Deep pink 'Bijou' Sweet Peas

Bushy forms of Sweet Peas range from low, spreading 'Cupid', which grows to only 6 in. tall, to 'Knee-Hi' and 'Jet Set', both of which grow to 36 in. Most bush strains are sold as mixtures of the full range of Sweet Pea colors.

WHERE TO PLANT

With different growth styles available, Sweet Peas can adorn the garden in any number of ways.

Traditional vining Sweet Peas make a colorful backdrop to perennials and low-growing shrubs. For dramatic exclamation points of color, train vines up one or more wire supports placed among other spring-blooming flowers.

Plant bush types in the foreground of beds. Place the self-supporting 'Explorer Mix', available in the full range of Sweet Pea shades, among late summer-blooming perennials for early color.

'Summer Breeze Mixed' peekin...

'Little Sweetheart' Sweet Peas

Containers are ideal for smaller bush-type Sweet Peas. You can grow Sweet Peas in windowboxes, mass them in large pots, or try them in hanging baskets.

PERFECT PARTNERS

Combine Sweet Peas with other summer flowers in red, blue, lilac, or white shades.

over a picket fence

For a sensory delight, plant low-growing 'Bijou Mixed' Sweet Peas with the taller, fragrant annual, Stock. Later-flowering, mixed-color 'Galaxy' Sweet Peas make an equally fragrant combination with Nicotianas.

Border a row of mixed-color 'Royal Family' Sweet Peas with low-growing 'Accord' Pansies in purple, blue, white, or yellow.

For stunning white and blue accents with the mixed colors of 24-30 in., early-blooming 'Continental' Sweet Peas, plant Candytuft, Lobelias, and Forget-me-nots.

'Russell Hybrid' Lupines prosper under the same conditions as 'Cuthbertson' Sweet Peas. Their spires offer a similar range of single or mixed colors, with the addition of yellow, but contrast in texture and form.

PLANTING & AFTERCARE

YOU WILL NEED: ❑ Sweet Pea seeds ❑ Garden fork ❑ Compost ❑ Support for vines ❑ Water

1 Prepare soil in fall. Dig a trench 12 in. wide and equally deep, and mix a generous amount of compost with soil in the trench.

2 Install a support for climbing before you plant seeds of vining types. Vine tendrils will cling to string or mesh.

3 Soak seeds in warm water for 24 hours before planting to aid sprouting. Germination takes two to three weeks.

4 Plant the seeds 1 in. deep in prepared soil. Space seeds 2 in. apart. Later, thin young plants to 6-12 in. apart.

5 Remove spent flowers regularly all season long. This prolongs the show of blooms by preventing plants from setting seed.

Tip

Apply a thin layer of mulch to vines once they are growing well, to help keep soil cool and to preserve moisture.

Secrets of Success

BUYING HINTS

- **Buy fresh seeds** that are packaged for planting in the current year (as marked on the seed packet).
- **Avoid buying seeds** too late in the season, when planting in hot weather could interfere with the vines' development.

SUN & SOIL

- **Full sun.** Sweet Peas need plenty of light for growth, plus good air circulation to keep diseases from troubling the foliage.
- **Rich, well-drained soil.** Plants need a regular supply of moisture, but they cannot take soggy soil.

SPECIAL ADVICE

- **Erect free-standing** trellises on a north-south axis, so that plants receive sun throughout the day.
- **In cooler climates,** plant Sweet Peas in fall, before frost. Dig a trench that is $1/2$-2 ft. long and deep. Plant seeds 2 in. deep.

 Seasonal Tips

FALL
Preparing soil
Dig and amend soil in the site that you intend to grow Sweet Peas in next year.

WINTER— EARLY SPRING
Planting
Sow seeds for blooms in spring and summer. Protect seedlings from pecking birds with wire mesh *(right)*.

SPRING—SUMMER
Maintaining
Keep plants well watered. Mulch plantings to conserve

moisture. Fertilize Sweet Pea plants on a monthly basis with a complete fertilizer. Regularly remove all faded flowers and developing seedpods from plants.

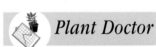 *Plant Doctor*

Powdery mildew is a fungal disease that appears as gray to white, powdery patches on leaves and stems. Severe infestations seriously weaken plants. Spray infested plants with an appropriate fungicide to protect uninfected new growth.

Tuberous Begonias

Luminous blooms to light up shady spots

Season	Special Features	Best Conditions
✳ Flowers from early summer to fall frost	✓ Easy to grow	⊕ Zones 2-10
❋ Repeat bloomer	✿ Fairly disease resistant	☀ Partial to full shade
		⬟ Well-drained, rich, moist soil

Height: 10-36 in.

Spread: 8-16 in.

Continuous Color Extravaganza

Adorn porches and beds all summer with the blooms of repeat-flowering Tuberous Begonias.

COLORS & VARIETIES

Tuberous Begonias sprout thick stems from a hairy, brown tuber and produce glossy or velvety, heart-shaped leaves. The emerald foliage is set off by glowing hues of large, single or double flowers. Shapes of different Tuberous Begonia flowers can resemble Roses, Camellias, or Carnations.

The impresive Camellia-flowered Begonias have double flowers up to 6 in. across on handsome, upright plants. The Picotee types have contrasting bands along the edges of scalloped, pink, red, or apricot petals.

Hybrid Miniatures and 'Non-Stop' types form attractive, bushy mounds covered with 1-2 in., Rose-shaped blooms in bright yellow, orange, red, or pink.

Cascade Begonias will arch gracefully from hanging baskets. 'Crimson Cascade' is a strong performer with rich

Ruffled 'Sunburst' Picotee

red blooms on long, trailing stems. Other Cascade colors include shades of pink, rose, gold, bright yellow, white, and pale tints with a deeper color at the petals' edges.

WHERE TO PLANT

These bold plants make a strong statement in any sheltered position. Be sure to give them a prominent place to showcase their exotic, tropical beauty.

In hanging baskets or windowboxes, Cascade Begonias will add glamour to east- or north-facing walls with their trailing stems that spill bouquets of bloom over the edges of containers.

For masses of color, plant Camellia-flowered Begonias in groups of three to five in front of shrubs. The cool green background will provide the perfect setting for the jewel-like hues of the blossoms.

Decorate outdoor seating areas with pots of

'Non-Stop Mixed' vibrate agar

Miniature or 'Non-Stop' Begonias. Or, tuck them into shady corners around a patio or pool for stunning accents.

PERFECT PARTNERS

Combine Tuberous Begonias with other shade-loving plants. Try planting them for summer color in areas where spring bulbs, such as Tulips, have finished flowering.

Camellia-flowered Begonia types blend well with Impatiens, which provide a nice contrast in both flowers and foliage. Try striking, cream-and-red 'Royal Picotee' Begonias with pink or white Impatiens.

Plant feathery Cinnamon or Ostrich Ferns against the

An orange 'Non-Stop' Begonia

a backdrop of Aucuba

foundation of your house as a backdrop for the bright orange 'City of Ballarat'. This arresting combination seems to glow in the shade.

Coordinate the salmon, pink-tinged 'Roy Hartley' with fuchsia-splashed Coleus to create an exciting tropical display edging a shady patio.

Cascades in a container

PLANTING & AFTERCARE

YOU WILL NEED: ❑ Begonia tubers ❑ Light potting soil ❑ 4 in. pots ❑ 2 ft. stakes ❑ Twine

1 **In late winter,** fill pots with soil to 1 ½ in. from the top. Set a tuber, concave side up, in each pot and cover with ½ in. of soil.

2 **Water and place** in bright light, but not direct sun, at 70 degrees F. Keep soil moist, but do not allow soil to get soggy.

3 **After danger** of frost has passed, transplant into beds 8 in. apart, or group four Cascade Begonias together in a 10-12 in. basket.

4 **Fertilize monthly** with balanced fertilizer, such as water-soluble 20-20-20. Tie upright Begonia types to stakes. Remove spent blooms.

5 **After first frost,** dig up tubers with soil intact and dry for a week indoors. Remove tops and soil; store in cool, dry peat or sand.

Troubleshooter

Begonias are highly susceptible to rot if tubers or stems remain wet. Water the soil around the plant, rather than the central crown.

Secrets of Success

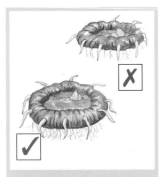

BUYING HINTS

- **Buy firm tubers.** Size does not determine flower quality but larger tubers may produce more blooms.
- **Avoid tubers** that look shrunken or shriveled. Do not buy potted plants in full bloom in spring; they may stop flowering by summer.

SUN & SOIL

- **No strong sun.** Sun in early morning or late afternoon will increase flowering, but midday sun can burn leaves.
- **Rich, moist soil.** Add well-rotted compost or peat moss to soil before planting Tuberous Begonias outside.

SPECIAL ADVICE

- **Remove the small,** insignificant female blossoms so that Tuberous Begonias can put more energy into developing showier male flowers.
- **When tying** upright Begonias, use soft twine or raffia and make loose ties.

 ## Seasonal Tips

LATE WINTER
Planting
Start Tuberous Begonias in pots indoors before planting outside to allow for good root development.

LATE SPRING
Transplanting
Transplant Tuberous Begonias to their summer positions. They should begin blooming in a few weeks.

SUMMER
Maintaining
Water and fertilize. Keep the plants well groomed by removing any spent blooms and dead leaves.

FALL
Storing
Dig up tubers *(below)* with some soil still attached. Let dry, then clean and store in a cool, frost-free place.

 ## Plant Doctor

Powdery mildew is the only disease that usually affects Tuberous Begonias. This flour-like fungus draws moisture out of the plants' leaves and buds, causing them to curl up and die. To prevent mildew, keep plants well watered and provide good air circulation.

The Essential
GARDEN ALMANAC

Creative Container Gardens

Arranging a bowl of flowers
in the morning can give a sense
of quiet in a crowded day—
like writing a poem or saying a prayer.

—*Anne Morrow Lindbergh*

WATER WANDS or automatic misters can ease the task of watering hanging baskets, especially if your basket plants are in high, hard-to-reach locations.

DURING THE HEAT of the summer, soil polymers, available at garden centers, can help retain water in containers that are placed in sunny locations. Add the polymers to the soil at the time you pot the plants rather than trying to mix it in later.

IF YOU ARE GOING to be away from your containers when they will need watering, you may want to invest in an automatic watering device. An inexpensive version can be made by filling a small (12-oz.) plastic soda bottle with water, placing your finger over the opening, turning it upside down, and quickly inserting the opening under the surface of the soil. Practice the technique outside with a soil-filled pot first. This works because the water will slowly seep into the soil over a period of several days.

MINERAL SALT DEPOSITS can build up on the soil's surface if you are overfertilizing, giving your container plants water with a high mineral content, or watering frequently with too little water. If you discover these white, powdery deposits, try periodically using distilled water or giving more water less frequently to wash these salts through the soil and out the bottom of the container.

FERTILIZING CONTAINER POTS can be a tricky process. The best solution is to use a slow-release fertilizer, which will ensure that your plants receive the nutrients that they need to grow vigorously but don't have a salty buildup.

Nature's Way

Most spring bulbs require a cold
treatment known as "vernalization"
in order to flower. Force spring bulbs
by planting them in containers
in the fall; place containers in a handy,
cool place outdoors for eight weeks, and
then bring indoors for winter blooms.

December
❑ Clean old pots and tubs to get them ready for spring planting.
❑ Repair or discard broken containers.
❑ Chill spring bulbs in warm regions.

January
❑ Bring forcing pots of spring bulbs indoors.
❑ Start Tuberous Begonias indoors.

February
❑ Bring more forcing pots of spring bulbs indoors.
❑ Start spring-flowering annuals indoors.

March
❑ Visit garden centers located in warm regions for the best selection of container plants.
❑ Repot spring- and summer-flowering plants.

April
❑ Visit garden centers located in cool regions for best selection of container plants.
❑ Propagate your Chrysanthemums and other fall-blooming container plants.

May
❑ Plant windowboxes and other outside containers.
❑ Fertilize your summer- and fall-blooming container plants.
❑ Purchase summer hanging baskets from nurseries and garden centers.

June
❑ Check container plants grown outside on daily basis to be sure they are getting enough moisture.
❑ Start Ornamental Kale seeds.

July
❑ Make faux stone containers.
❑ Prune back late-spring flowering plants.
❑ Pinch back fall-flowering plants to increase flowers.

August
❑ Be sure that your outdoor container plants are getting sufficient water during this hot month.

September
❑ Purchase fall-blooming container plants from garden centers and nurseries.
❑ Move tender container plants indoors for winter.

October
❑ Move tender tubers and bulbs indoors before frost.
❑ Repot your spring-flowering plants.
❑ Before first frost, make Geranium cuttings for overwintering in pots.

November
❑ Plant spring bulbs in pots for forcing. Place them in a cool location.
❑ Start Paperwhite Narcissus in pots for holiday gift-giving.

INDEX

INDEX

INDEX